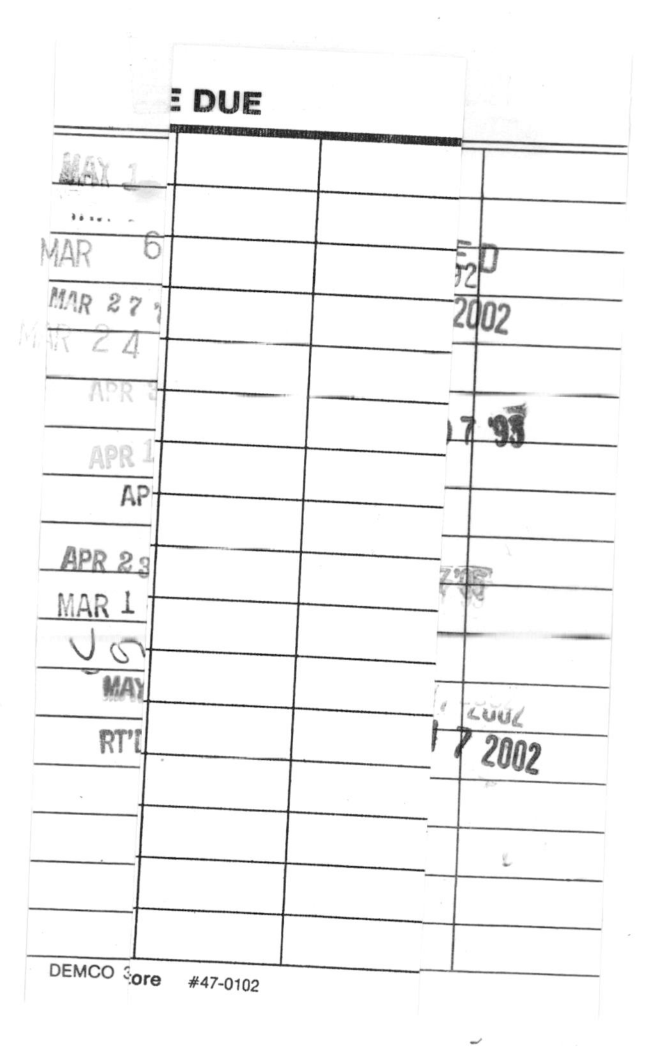

Maternal Bereavement

Maternal Bereavement

Coping With the Unexpected Death of a Child

Linda Edelstein

PRAEGER SPECIAL STUDIES • PRAEGER SCIENTIFIC

New York • Philadelphia • Eastbourne, UK
Toronto • Hong Kong • Tokyo • Sydney

Library of Congress Cataloging in Publication Data

Edelstein, Linda.
Maternal bereavement.

Includes bibliographical references and index.
1. Children—Death—Psychological aspects. 2. Mother and child. 3. Bereavement—Psychological aspects. 4. Mothers—Psychology. I. Title.
BF575.G7E33 1984 155.9'37 83-21124
ISBN 0-03-063908-5 (alk. paper)

Published in 1984 by Praeger Publishers
CBS Educational and Professional Publishing
a Division of CBS Inc.
521 Fifth Avenue, New York, NY 10175 USA

456789 052 98765432

Printed in the United States of America
on acid-free paper

To the loving memory of my parents

Sarah Pozner Edelstein
and
Jack Edelstein

Preface

There has been an increased clinical and research emphasis in recent years on the mourning-liberation process, a universal transformational process related to the adaptation to loss and change. Initially the distinction between the mourning process and its subcategory, bereavement—the reaction to the death of a significant other—was not made. We now know this differentiation is useful in that it allows us to understand many aspects of loss and change that do not follow an external death. In addition, more contemporary clinical research is now investigating specific losses in order to further elucidate the meaning of the "lost" object to the individual confronted with the mourning situation. In my own work, I find this latter research especially helpful when combined with a developmental perspective.

Dr. Edelstein's monograph is a major contribution to the growing body of empirical research findings. She has addressed issues of the mourning-liberation process, bereavement, and specifically has systematically gathered pertinent data on the adaptations of mothers to the deaths of their children. Her work eloquently speaks for itself. Many of her findings and conclusions are consonant with my own research and clinical experience. She has effectively reviewed the pertinent literature in the field, integrated knowledge and interpretation, and has presented her findings and conclusions in a clear and lucid manner. I am especially pleased that Dr. Edelstein has included in her study the social contexts of the bereavement process. These do have healing significance although the intrapsychic components, I believe, are of the greatest importance in the adaptive process. Shared experiences may help, but individual pain must be dealt with internally.

In my research I have found the mourning-bereavement process in mothers who have lost children through death is rarely fully completed. There is some liberation but not as total in response to other significant deaths. However, there can still be creative outcomes despite the incompleteness of the process, e.g., Kaethe Kollwitz.

Dr. Edelstein's work can be read with great benefit by many different readers, e.g., mental health professionals, social scientists, physicians, the clergy, and by those human beings who have had the unfortunate loss she writes about. It is a privilege to be able to introduce this work.

George H. Pollock, M.D., Ph.D.
President
Institute for Psychoanalysis, Chicago

November, 1983

Acknowledgments

I found that writing this book was, in many ways, an easier task than trying to put words to my deep feelings of affection and appreciation for the people who have been so important to me during these three years of research and writing.

An earlier version of this book was supported by my doctoral dissertation committee at Northwestern University: Solomon Cytrynbaum, Ph.D., Fay Lomax Cook, Ph.D., Margaret Lee, Ph.D., and Janet Stern, M.A., who worked with me in the best spirit of cooperation and scholarship. Mary Bucholtz typed that early version and Mary Ann Gariti had the good nature and skill to type a later one.

During the research and writing, I had my own support system—three marvelous friends and talented colleagues: Carol Gaston, M.S., Debra Gilbert, M.Ed., and Joanne Marengo, Ph.D., who provided essential insights, criticism, emotional support and statistical advice. At a significant point of decision, I was lucky to receive generous encouragement from George Pollock, M.D. Ph.D., whose work in the area of adaptation has been influential on my own efforts. Then, too, George Zimmar, senior psychology editor at Praeger, was receptive and enthusiastic in working with me to ready the final manuscript. The last draft was read by Joan Gold, M.S. and William Alexy, Ph.D. Coming from different perspectives, their careful reading and thoughtful criticisms found mistakes that I was too close to see.

There are other people whose influence has been felt consistently throughout the thinking and writing of this book. My respect and gratitude goes to James Fisch, M.D., who gave me confidence because of his special understanding of the work on the page and between the lines. My deepest thanks go to the women whose story I have tried to tell. They spoke with me and wrote to me, having so much to teach and share. In doing so, they reaffirmed my faith in the strength of the individual spirit. Lastly, my love and thanks to Keira and Jennifer, my daughters, whose boundless capacity for loving saw us through some difficult days.

—•—

Contents

Part Two

—•—

List of Tables and Figures

LIST OF FIGURES

LIST OF TABLES

Maternal Bereavement

Part One

one

Introduction

How do women adapt to a major loss? This study steps in at the middle of lives that have been unexpectedly disrupted by one of life's most devastating losses: the death of a child. This work joins others that have attempted to understand the process of bereavement and the gradual adaptation to lives so suddenly changed. With these women and the reader, I explore the experiences subsequent to the death as the women attempt to cope with a tragedy that has assaulted their identities and precipitated a major life crisis.

A blend of quantitative and qualitative research strategies was used in going about this work. The nature of the bereavement process ultimately dictated the types of methodology, respecting the nature of the internal and external worlds under study. The objective, from the start, was to learn about the experience of women whose older children, not infants, had died without warning. With this in mind, the study developed as a compromise between reaching many impersonally by using survey methods, or reaching fewer women more intimately through individual talks.

The variables of whether or not there are remaining children, the ages of the mother and child, the cause of death, and the preparation time preceding the death have consistently been considered significant in affecting the mourning process. For that reason, it was decided to interview a homogeneous group to explore the dynamics of the process, and to survey a larger, diverse number only about the use of social and emotional support.

THE WOMEN

> I was prepared to be honest. You got more out of me, and I knew I was going to tell you more than I'd tell anyone because I feel that society will not let me grieve normally. I wish there was a ritual—they could chop off your finger or something—to express your grief. . . . They don't let you, they don't let you . . . and I don't blame them. I wouldn't either. If this were not my hand dealt to me, I would not touch this with a ten-foot pole.
>
> (Anne, 1 year later)

Even after deciding some of the things to ask, I did not know how to find women who would talk to me—the loss had been so great. I imagined that the adjustment would be equally difficult—reasons that had drawn me to try to understand the process, but made me all the more uneasy about approaching people.

Compassionate Friends, Inc., was contacted. This is an international organization that describes itself as a "self-help organization offering friendship and understanding to bereaved parents."[1] The individuals there had respect for research and were enthusiastic about supporting any work that would educate the general public about the magnitude of child loss.

The names of chapter leaders were freely given, and the authorization to pursue my inquiries was willingly granted, as long as the rights and privacy of individuals were respected. Several chapter leaders were contacted and agreed to mail out questionnaires with requests for interviews in the monthly newsletter. The mailing lists are large, confidential, compiled from various sources, and include many people who never affiliate with Compassionate Friends in any other way. The newsletters are also unsolicited, so they reach people who may or may not have welcomed receiving them or the questionnaires.

The questionnaires went out blindly. The advantages to this large mailing outweighed the disadvantages. It provided a clearer sociodemographic picture of many bereaved mothers, including those who could not be personally interviewed; it gathered information on the use of social and emotional supports from a large number of individuals; it identified the people and kinds of help that women found useful during this period; and it was a means of requesting an interview.

In all, 130 responses were received, a return rate of 21.2 percent. This is an expectable return for a sensitive topic, especially one contained in an unknown and unsolicited mailing.[2] The final number of completed questionnaires included was 127, with 72 (56.7 percent) responses from women who were categorized as occasional or frequent self-help group members, and 55 (43.3 percent) from women who rarely or never used Compassionate Friends. From these responses, the women to be interviewed were sought.

The interview group was to be fairly homogeneous along certain significant criteria. The women were to be white, middle class, over 34 years old at the time of the child's death, under 60 years old presently, and to have other living children. The deaths were all of children over the age of nine (the average age was 17 years), unexpected, and not an obvious suicide. The specifics for the ages of mother and child were in an effort to reach women well into the mothering role and even, perhaps, women who had decided not to have any more children. There has been increased attention paid to child loss in recent years, but it has been primarily about the deaths occurring at birth or in infancy. This study, concentrating on the deaths of older children, does not imply that mothers who have lost younger children are suffering less or recovering easily. The emphasis on older mothers and children was simply in an effort to do justice to some of the particular issues faced by them. The same is true of race and gender. Race became a factor because the locations of the mailings reached few nonwhites. Bereaved fathers and siblings are only tangentially addressed here, yet they are other groups deserving of greater attention. It is because all these groups are, in some ways, special and unique that they cannot be blended together. They must be respected for their differences, as well as the similarities, in their experiences during mourning.

All the women who met these criteria and had indicated a willingness to be interviewed were contacted. All but one (just remarried after many years) accepted. Seven were members of Compassionate Friends and nine were not. The group of sixteen women turned out to be, as compared with all questionnaire respondents, older (mean of 45.6 years compared to 37.5 years), better educated (most having completed college, as compared with some college), having higher family incomes, more often married, more often Protestant, and more often working outside the home. The interrelatedness of some of these characteristics, such as work, marriage, and education, to income is no surprise. Tables detailing and comparing these distributions are included in the Appendix (see Tables 1, 2, and 3).

Most interviews were held at the women's homes so I was able to share in pictures and other important remembrances of these womens' lives. Several husbands joined the meeting, usually very quietly, walking in and out, waiting until the formal interviewing was over before asking questions and giving their opinions. I was often reminded by the wives, and came to realize it strongly, that their husbands were the more ignored individuals—women tended to receive more interest and concern than men. They also felt that social customs and relationships restricted the men's grieving more than their own. Interviews varied in length from 1-½ hours to 2-½ hours. In every instance, the women were open and gracious in talking with a stranger, although a few were surprised that anyone would want to hear about the death. ("If I didn't have to be here, I wouldn't come near me.") They needed to talk, they wanted others to know their child, they were eager to teach and educate anyone who genuinely wanted to learn about their experience, and they wanted to see research that they hoped would reach other people.

The mothers differed in their desire and ability to discuss the events and feelings. The interviews differed greatly in tone and emphasis, although similar questions were asked in each. The women are quoted throughout this book and the stories are theirs. To insure anonymity, many details have been changed. The stories have their own power without identifying information.

Whether their experience can be generalized to men, other racial, socioeconomic or cultural groups, is questionable. I came to believe that the underlying dynamics are universal—and can teach us about adaptation in general—but the uniqueness of each individual's personality, history, coping styles, relationships, and circumstances make every story painfully new.

THE METHODS

> I don't know where it fits in on graphs and tables and things, and you can't—I hope to God—you can't do that sort of research for this kind of question.
>
> (Deborah)

The interviews and talks formed the primary basis for this study. These taped and transcribed conversations were designed to elicit a description of the woman's experience of the death, her mourning, and the events and feelings of that time. It was both the behavioral and subjective components that were sought. The open-ended questions provided a frame of reference without placing restraint on her responses, thereby encouraging freedom to explain. Unsolicited responses and volunteered information were encouraged because they are excellent ways of getting information that had not been anticipated. The interviews also give flexibility, depth, and the ability to probe certain areas and new lines of thought.

There were also significant limitations to the interview. There are degrees of forgetting, not only resistance, particularly over time and in response to stressful events. This is true in any study, but as it pertains to the subject studied here, it is a dimension to remain aware of, especially in those interviews that took place several years after the death. Also, in gathering information there is the possibility that in recalling the event, the emotions that surrounded it may also reemerge and individuals may be distressed at revealing them. People differ in their tolerance for painful affect, in their needs and desires to discuss the death, and in their comfort with a stranger. Yet, the understanding of emotional material teaches us the meaning of this profound experience. Women who have been through the death of a child are intimate with strong emotions and, in some instances, there may have been less reluctance in expressing them to an interested professional than to friends or acquaintances. Deborah commented about her crying, "If you've been talking to mothers, you must be used to this."

In bringing back memories and emotions, unexpected gains were also apparent. The interviews allowed, for some, the additional perspective that comes with the passage of time. This gave rise to new insights and the ability to discuss some aspects of the experience that were forgotten or would have been too painful to discuss at the time.

The interviews form the heart of this work. But the questionnaire data on emotional and social supports provide another form of information. (A sample questionnaire appears in the Appendix.) There were also conversations with people who had experienced other types of loss and death, professionals who work with bereaved parents, and rich existing work in the field of grief that added to this book.

I have attempted, in the following chapters, to describe and interpret a range of subjective and behavioral phenomena. There are two parts to the book. Part One, Chapters Two through Six, follows the mother and her solitary absorption of the mourning process. Chapter Two, *Mourning and Bereavement,* reviews existing research about the process of mourning and adaptation to loss and death. These are fundamental concepts whose understanding we will pursue for the remainder of the book. The chapter includes an examination of the universality of the mourning process; the specifics of bereavement, a subcategory of mourning that refers to the reactions to death; and possible variations in the process; and psychological defense mechanisms.

Chapter Three, *The Mother/Child Relationship,* uses theory and case material to elucidate some dynamics of this special pair. It is only through an understanding of the meaning of the relationship between the mother and child that we can begin to examine what is lost. This chapter, then, builds the necessary contextual surroundings. It includes views on maternal feelings and behaviors, primarily from the psychoanalytic viewpoint; the meaning of having a child; and the personal illusions held by mothers. It calls attention to the uniqueness of each relationship by showing the actual dynamics of mothers and children at different points in life.

Chapter Four, *Disorganization,* describes the early days and weeks of the mothers' mourning. The initial impact, the numbness, the passivity and plans, and those awful early weeks are explained by the women themselves. This is the beginning, as the realization of the death slowly begins to be understood. The vivid dynamics of this period is testimony to the difficulty in believing that the loved child no longer exists.

Chapter Five, *Holding On/Letting Go*—The Struggle, continues to follow the process of mourning. As the initial coping mechanisms such as numbness and disbelief decrease, the woman is increasingly immersed in a lengthy, intense struggle of relinquishing the child as a living member of the family.

Chapter Six, *Reorganization,* traces the mothers' progress in their later stage of bereavement. Mourning for a child goes on indefinitely, but the adaptive mechanisms used to deal with this loss change over time. This chapter follows the women for as long as six years after the death as they rebuild their lives. It includes starting back (approximately after the first year); looking for new directions in their lives (approximately after the second year); acceptance of the permanence of the loss and change (during the third year); and integrating the past with the future (from the fourth year onward).

Part Two brings in many of the other people who are also touched by the death. Chapter Seven, *Emotional and Social Supports: Family and Friends,* looks at a different aspect of the bereavement. Although the focus is on the mother, she is not alone in the tragedy. This chapter examines the impact of the death on her relationships with the other members of her family and friends during the first year or two of bereavement. The question of who is helpful to these women is explored, and we draw upon the questionnaire data to form hypotheses. Chapter Eight, *Emotional and Social Supports: Professionals and a Self-help Group,* addresses relationships with professionals; different thoughts about intervention in normal and pathological bereavement; and the uses of Compassionate Friends, Inc.

Chapter Nine, *Rethinking the Problem,* pursues an understanding of prior losses as a significant factor in adaptation; disagreement with previous theories about loss; substantiation of others; and guides for conceptualizing major losses in women's lives.

This book is not written for any one group of readers. In thinking about colleagues and students who would read it and add to research and theory, I have included some of the rationale behind my thinking, method, and procedures, as well as the statistical data in the Appendix. For professionals, too, I have tried to provide an adequate review of the literature on important topics and dynamics, with extensive footnotes. Chapter Eight is especially designed for those whose work brings them into contact with mourning adults, not only bereaved mothers. In general, I have written for any interested reader.

The question asked most frequently of me was, "Why study bereaved mothers?" It has taken several years to understand even some of the answers to that question and it must suffice to say that I wanted to understand some of the different paths taken after this devastating loss. From these special women, I learned a great deal about the quiet courage of bereavement and adaptation.

It is out of respect to the individuals who struggle through bereavement and my colleagues who try to be there with them that for most of this book I have allowed, even encouraged, the emotion, pain, and intensity of mourning to live on these pages.

NOTES

1. Compassionate Friends, Inc. national headquarters is located at P.O. Box 1347, Oak Brook, IL 60521.

2. Morton Lieberman, "The Effects of Social Supports on Responses to Stress," in *Handbook of Stress,* ed. L. Goldberger and S. Breznitz (New York: Free Press, 1981). Sherman and Lieberman received a response rate of 30 percent when surveying bereaved parents, the lowest return of their five self-help group samples.

two

Mourning and Bereavement

MOURNING

> I thought I wasn't going to be able to handle it. I thought I couldn't face reality and would go on living as I did before.
>
> (Sandy)

Mourning is an adaptive process which includes reactions to loss as well as readjustment to an external environment that has changed.[1] The process of mourning has been identified clearly as a response to the loss of a loved person, and also to an abstraction that has a meaning equivalent to a loved one, for example, one's ideals or homeland.[2]

As an essential concept used throughout this book, mourning is conceived of as having evolved as a means of dealing with change as well as loss.[3] ". . . as one passes from childhood into adulthood, friends, lovers, and often family members are separated. Changes in residence, occupation, or place of business often entail separations. Even important successes in life—promotion, graduation, marriage—at the same time confront one with separation and loss."[4] Because all change involves the "loss" of something, it entails a modified process of mourning that may never be understood as such, even by the person. The losses may be compensated for by gains and never become troublesome, although it is not unusual for successes to also produce disruptive reactions.

The work of mourning is a struggle in which repeated testing of reality shows the individual that the loved person no longer exists in the external world. This requires that energy be withdrawn from its attachment to the child. It is a process that includes reluctant and gradual decathexis. The internal work is adjusting to reality. Because loss and change upset the individual equilibrium, mourning is the transitional period needed to reestablish a modified equilibrium based on a changed reality. Mourning is an example of adaptation, that striving toward acceptable compromise with life, neither total triumph over the environment nor total surrender to it.[5] When viewed as reactions and adaptation to loss and change, mourning can be seen as occurring continuously throughout life.

Work in the areas of psychology, sociology, and religion has referred to mourning subsequent to losses other than death: relocation after moving or losing a home due to slum clearance efforts; after major surgery and, more particularly, after amputation of a limb; subsequent to a flood that devastated a small mountain community, and other disasters; resulting from separation and divorce; following rape and abortion; and after the loss of sexual function in women.[6]

Less tangible losses that have activated the mourning process have been noted as occurring during the introspective work of therapy and after the loss of symptoms or a hope.[7] Recently, too, mourning has been identified as a component of aging, when one becomes aware of "what might have been," and at life transitions such as adolescence and midlife.[8]

These are only some of the different types of loss that may evoke a mourning process. What is it, then, that is lost and requires adaptation in the form of mourning? Different types of loss can be conceptualized, but they are not distinct or mutually exclusive. They are: (1) the loss of a loved or valued person, either permanently or temporarily; (2) loss of health, attitudes, or social roles; (3) loss of external objects such as money, home or homeland; and (4) those developmental losses occurring during the process of growth.[9]

The significant commonality is the experience that an aspect of one's self is lost:

> I had this feeling that I am never going to be the same person. And I don't think I ever will be. . . . It just seems like Larry will be right there forever. . . . It doesn't seem like it is he who will ever fade. I

might . . . Everything is before Larry died and after Larry died . . . My life seems to be split up into two sections that way.

(Louise, 1-¾ years later)

BEREAVEMENT

Goofy stages, goofy feelings that you can't explain and that you don't care if you do or not.

(Sandy)

Bereavement, the reaction to the death of a loved person, is a subcategory of the mourning process but the clearest to conceptualize in terms of loss.

Much of the theoretical work on the process of mourning is an extension of the work on bereavement. Many of the assumptions about loss without death are based on the theories about bereavement. Reactions to death have been a perpetual concern of man, but only recently have been studied systematically in terms of stages, affects, and outcomes. The remainder of this chapter reviews bereavement research and theory that address stages, atypical reactions, and psychological defenses.

Bereavement normally proceeds through stages, each playing a distinct part in the work. Each stage is accompanied by many different feelings, but some tend to predominate and, as such, are indicators of the intrapsychic work in progress. The normal course of bereavement results in freeing energy for reinvestment in productive endeavors.

Stages in Bereavement

In the 1930s, work began to point to stages in the process. Later researchers were able to more clearly distinguish a sequential development with predominant types of affect and intensity of emotion.[10] Different theorists have found more similarities than differences in the sequential nature and description of the process. Although the generally accepted two-stage model is summarized in Table 2-1, the process here was clearer to conceptualize in the three stages of Table 2-2. This appears to be due to two reasons. First, the unexpectedness of the death dramatically intensified the first phase, the initial impact and disorganization, encouraging that period to be isolated artificially as a distinct stage. Second, the death of a child precipitates such a lengthy intense mourning period, there is much to look at and try to understand. Breaking down and organizing the process provides a way of grappling with complexities. Both tables convey the process as including rebuilding as the final task, not possible without the work of the other stages.

TABLE 2-1. Stages and Affects in the Mourning Process.

Stage	*Phase*	*Associated Affect*
Acute	Shock	Numbness, disbelief, shrieking, motor retardation
	Searching	Yearning for the lost object, weeping
	Grief reactions	Despair, sadness, depression, fatigue, helplessness
	Separation reactions	Anger, anxiety
Chronic	Reintegration	Acceptance of loss

Conceptualizing a process into stages has its pitfalls. It tends to communicate ways that people *should* feel and adapt. This is certainly not the goal here. Adaptation to major loss is a complex, often emotionally overwhelming process. A conceptual framework is intended to provide, for the parent, student, or helping professional, a way to begin to manage the unmanageable, to guide, to reduce anxiety, and to signal the need for professional intervention.

It is useful, before addressing the specifics of the bereaved mothers in this study, to briefly review the stages and affective reactions found

TABLE 2-2. Stages and Affects in Maternal Bereavement.

Stage	*Major Dynamics*
Disorganization	Disruption in the equilibrium as a result of trauma
(Early Days	Acclimating period)
Holding on/Letting go	Struggle to relinquish the child as living; retaining memories and identification
Reorganization	Modified equilibrium resulting in an alliance with the past and ongoing activities; loss is integrated into life

by others and compare their findings to the general dynamics of maternal bereavement. The researchers summarized here have drawn their conclusions from bereavement,[11] from mourning in general,[12] and from a variety of losses occurring after natural disasters.[13]

There is general agreement that mourning begins with an initial shock reaction, including numbness and disbelief. The shock is the impact felt from excessive stimulation due to the awareness that cannot be integrated. It has been compared to emotional terror, caused by a sudden loss of control over internal or external reality, or both.[14] Similarly, observers who studied reactions after a flood wiped out rural communities of Buffalo Creek, West Virginia, understood shock as a blow to the psyche that breaks through one's defenses so suddenly and with such brutal force that one cannot react effectively.[15]

Shock

Shock varies in intensity with the suddenness or preparation for the loss. It may include shrieking, moaning, and motor retardation. The length of the shock is usually very short, marking the awareness of threatened security. For these mothers, the shock marked the beginning of the stage of Disorganization, increased by the unexpectedness of the loss. They had no time to anticipate the death or subsequent events.

Anticipation would have provided a period of rehearsal and time to begin to acclimate themselves to the idea.

Searching

The phenomena of pining and searching have been documented as following the shock reaction. They indicate a yearning for the lost person and attempts to recover him or her. The interesting point has been made that it is not only the other person that is lost, but there is also the experience of being lost one's self.[16]

The emotions throughout this time seem to occur in episodic bursts, rather than with consistency. The awareness of the loss sweeps through similarly to the first awareness, bringing emotions in waves. Weeping, different from the wailing or moaning seen during shock, may indicate an attempt at reunion because crying has its roots in early mother/child interactions when the infant's cry brought the mother's presence. The weeping, searching, and pining imply that there is still hope.

For bereaved mothers, the pining and searching begin in the Early Days and continue, diminishing in intensity, throughout the struggle of Holding on/Letting go. Residue of this yearning may go on indefinitely.

There is evidence that the unexpectedness of death also increases the time spent in searching activity and hopefulness. Expecting the death enables mourners to give up attempting to recover the dead person more quickly than those people who were unprepared for the loss.

In the course of this work, it became apparent that these women had a strong desire to know more and to find answers. Most of the women were not satisfied by easy answers or quick solutions but were engaged in a search to make sense out of some, if not all, of the experience. They were all knowledgeable about grief and had read many books on death and dying, had talked to others, and attended workshops and groups. Some had thoroughly investigated their child's death, reading accident reports and talking to people who had information about it. They were impressive in their interest in learning more about what had happened to them and the meaning of it. This is partly a result of the death being sudden and unexpected. They had no time to prepare and satisfy themselves with reasons. The mothers never really understood *why.*

Grief reactions

Grief reactions, the next phase of the process, is the time of realizing that nothing can undo the loss. This is a time of despair, sadness, and depression. Fatigue and exhaustion are also common symptoms, as are lethargy, weakness, emptiness, and disorganized behavior. The sorrow and helplessness reflect an awareness of the finality of the loss. These affects are seen most clearly in the struggle of Holding on/Letting go, engaging most mothers intensely for at least a year and slowly diminishing after that time.

The awareness of the loss, which is part of the grief reactions, changes into an acceptance of reality in the separation reactions.

Separation reactions

As the grief reactions fade into separation reactions, anger and anxiety are noted. The anger is a result of being left, implying that the loss is recognized and acknowledged. A dissenting view posits anger as a feature of the early yearning and the loss of aggressiveness as an indicator of despair.[17] Anxiety is the response to the full realization of the death and threat to one's security. The struggle of Holding on/Letting go includes these important dynamics.

The period of separation reactions marks the subtle shift from the acute to the chronic stage in mourning, Reintegration.

Reintegration

The chronic stage begins when the initial adaptive mechanisms increase in an attempt to integrate the experience of the loss with reality.[18] It has also been called Reintegration or Reorganization, both implying decathexis with a reinvestment in life activities. During the chronic stage, the affect is not dramatic and behavioral functioning is generally as it was or reorganized. The Holding on/Letting go stage, because it goes on so long in child loss, has some aspects of the chronic stage of bereavement, but cannot be viewed as identical to reorganization. For bereaved mothers, full reinvestment in life and its activities is a hard-won battle, happening slowly and filled with setbacks.

No longitudinal studies exist to document the entire mourning process. Most prior research concentrates on the dramatic impact of the first year. From this group of women, all at least 11 months away from the death, and several 4 years or more away, more insights into the course of the process and the subtle dynamics of adaptation can be gained.

Outcomes and Atypical Reactions in Bereavement

Reintegration or reorganization, although the optimal outcome, is not the only possible resolution in bereavement. There are also a variety of possible deviations to the process. The numerous pathological possibilities for mourning include: inhibited, delayed or absent grief; chronic grief; depression; exacerbation of previous conditions or new illness; acting out; and neurotic and psychotic reactions. In the following, all atypical reactions, there is a component of strong but only partially successful attempts to avoid grieving.[19]

1. Inhibited, delayed, or absent grief may reflect a relationship in which the loss is not strongly felt, personal values about the appearance and show of emotions connected with loss, an extended period of shock, or postponement of affect until it cannot be avoided. This does not necessarily reflect pathology.

> I handled it rather well. Maybe that's not true (laugh). As I'm saying this, I'm also thinking of all the days that I wasn't able to get out of bed . . . . Maybe I did a good job of, of putting on a good appearance for the outside world . . . I come from a stoic background.
>
> (Marion)

But there are a number of individuals who neither show nor are aware of feelings associated with mourning. They may be struggling with intense ambivalence and are afraid of what they will reveal. Observations of cases in which there was a complete absence of mourning reactions usually attribute it to the results of strong early attempts to overcome hostility toward the lost person. It now creates great difficulties in experiencing the normal range of emotions, including hostility or anger. Others have found ambivalence or conflicting emotions, more than positive ties, to be the important factor in intense mourning reactions.[20] It makes it difficult for the mourner to freely express the emotions connected to the death. Delayed, inhibited, or absent grief is considered to make an individual more vulnerable to anniversary reactions.

2. Chronic grief is closely related to inhibited, delayed, or absent grief because it is also a defense against the bereavement process. It is a different form serving the same purpose—not letting go of the person—and not completing the mourning which would result in a changed attachment. This is most clearly shown in behavior patterns that deny the change in reality (e.g., in cases of bereavement, retaining a room or possessions exactly as they were prior to the loss).

3. Unmanifested grief will be expressed to the full in one way or another. Severe unmotivated depressions may be the subsequent expression of withheld emotional reactions. Depression is an inhibited response to loss and differs from sadness. Depression is, to some extent, a protest denying the loss and retaining the hope of undoing it. It is also a response to something often impersonal and diffuse. Sadness, on the other hand, is seen as a confession acknowledging personal yearning, the rage of which is against the acknowledged loss. The hope of undoing the loss is gone, and it is a response to specific rather than diffuse loss.[21]

Lifton notes that depression in grief is an identification with death itself. It is loss of an innocence in which one felt safer and more removed from death. Depression is, in part, a protest directed at everything associated with loss.

> What the protest seems to be saying is: We are defeated, inwardly dead, helpless, but we do not accept this state of things. We in fact cry out in pain, and perhaps in silence against our fate. We know of something better because we lived it in the past, and although we can hardly imagine a return to that privileged state prior to the loss, neither can we surrender it nor accept the actuality imposed upon us. What eats away at everyone in depression is not so much ambivalence toward the dead person, as Freud thought, as this terrible duality of simultaneous immersion in the deep sadness of irreplaceable loss and the perpetual ineffectual protest against that loss.[22]

Some depression is normal in the mourning process, and does not always reflect pathological significance. It becomes an atypical response through qualitative symptoms.

4. Hypochondriasis and exacerbation of preexisting somatic conditions allow the individual to concentrate on a physical concern rather than the loss and its consequences. It is often an elaboration of a symptom associated with mourning, or a symptom related to the dead person, one form of pathological identification.

> I would relive the whole thing emotionally again. I kept fainting . . . I woke up and the paramedics had come in. I thought I was dying. I just wanted (them) to go away and let me finish what I thought was dying . . . I was very upset that they had interrupted . . . I was happy I was going.
>
> (Anne)

It is, as are the other atypical reactions, a way of venting emotions, usually anxiety, hostility, and guilt, in this case through symptom formation. The body becomes the victim in an attempt to both expiate for and gratify the unacceptable wish. The individual gains attention and care at an enormous price. It has been proposed that situations of loss may precede the development of all types of illnesses if the individual is predisposed.[23]

The stress of mourning may also exacerbate preexisting conditions. This is different in that the individual does not respond to the symptoms as if they were a new and terrible disease. These reactions may occur more frequently in those individuals who have difficulty expressing feelings although they are aware of them. Increased physical pain appears to be more acceptable than the pain of loss.

Loss is generally accepted as a possible factor in the development of some medical symptoms, illness, and psychophysiologic reactions. Diseases that are specifically associated with loss are hypertension, ulcerative colitis, duodenal ulcer, and neurodermatitis, both in terms of pathogenesis and exacerbation.

It must be noted that it is not simply a matter of stimulus ⟶ response (loss event ⟶ illness). Personal predisposition, meaning of the loss, coping processes, and other factors influence whether, and to what degree, there will be a physiological reaction.

5. Acting out, handling strong internal feelings through action, is another reaction. As a response to loss, it can be seen in attempts to find immediate replacements for the lost object. This can be done through relationships, work, alcohol, or drug dependence. Substitution in an extreme way satisfies the emotions while denying them. For example, drugs can become the instant defense against the pain and resolution of the mourning process.

6. Forms of neurotic and psychotic reaction may be precipitated or made more severe by significant loss. Neurotics often exhibit anxiety states replacing mourning which can be understood as regressive, de-

rived from infantile anxiety in reaction to separation from protective and loving persons.

There are extreme reactions, such as suicide, which may result from a pathological identification with the dead. The reactions discussed here are, in the extreme, the atypical responses to loss. Some of these reactions are related to psychological defenses commonly associated with both pathological and normal bereavement. Defenses are essential to coping with loss, but can become pathological in the extreme, interfering with individual adjustment.[24]

Psychological Defenses in Bereavement

The death of a child is that kind of tragedy which calls on all of one's resources. The psychological defenses discussed here are those processes that allow the mourner to tolerate the shattering experience. They are inherent in mourning and are neither conscious nor voluntary. In this section some of those processes most commonly associated with adaptation to major loss are looked at.

Not surprisingly, denial is a primary mechanism of the early acute stage of mourning, although there is little agreement on at exactly which point in the process it is predominant. Denial is an attempt to turn away from the acknowledgment and acceptance of the loss, and implies an appraisal of the situation as being dangerous. The function of denial, in repudiating all or part of the meaning of the loss, is to reduce the emotional response, usually that of fear and anxiety. It is manifested in numerous ordinary ways such as setting a place at the table for the child or buying his or her favorite foods. More extreme versions of denial include preserving the child's room exactly as it was. Related to denial is avoidance or minimization, and there is a tendency to ascribe actions to denial when it is the more conscious dynamic of avoidance that is at work. Avoidance is manifested, for example, in the voluntary behavior of taking another route when driving in order to bypass the scene of the fatal accident.

Based on work with victims of Hiroshima, a phenomenon of "psychic numbing" has been documented as a response to severe trauma. Psychic numbing is a radical but temporary diminution in one's sense of actuality in order to avoid losing this sense altogether. It is tied to both denial and identification.[25] Denial is seen in the shutting down, the numbing as protection against a damaging awareness. Identification is allying oneself with the dead by experiencing a reversible and symbolic death.

As a defense in bereavement, identification with the dead person or aspects of him or her is argued by most writers, but not by all, to be crucial in the mourning process.[26] Identification, whether conscious or unconscious, accomplishes the modeling of the mourner's personality in the image of the one lost, insuring that the attachment continues. It is a way of holding on because identification with elements of the person means that he or she is never completely given up, but instead transformed into a part of one's self. An interesting question is raised by the issue of identification because the same group of theorists who argue that total decathexis is necessary also maintains that mourning cannot be completed without identification with the lost person. Identification and memories are usually considered the residue of the completed mourning process. This question may be answered by looking at Freud's early statement that mourning work "requires that all libido shall be withdrawn from its attachment to this object."[27] In later writing, he noted that withdrawal of the libido attached to one person can only take place when the lost person is "reinstated" within the ego.[28] It appears, then, that identification is central to the work of mourning as a process allowing libidinal decathexis through gradual internalization in the ego. People then are never "let go," but transformed from being held outside one's self to bringing aspects of them into the ego structure.

Identification can be developmental and adaptive. Used defensively in mourning, identification negates the loss, but in more maturational activity, identification can lead to increased adaptation to reality.

When the internal substitute replaces the externally severed relationship, increased individuality results. It is the outcome of setting boundaries between one's self and the world. The experience of loss and the establishment of boundaries are mutually constitutive because to experience loss the individual must have some degree of separateness, and the loss can further promote boundaries.[29] One thesis contends that in psychic reality the object is immortal and it therefore makes more sense to speak of various fates rather than object loss pure and simple. The three non-mutually exclusive fates are: establishment as introjects and other primary process presences; transformation into identifications which, to a degree, may take on the character of impersonalized systemic regulations; and preservation of the object such that it remains external to the subjective self. In the mourning process, where the emphasis falls influences whether, or to what degree, the process results in growth or stagnation.[30]

Altruism, another defense related to identification, is rarely mentioned in the studies of mourning, yet it is referred to in the descriptions of disasters and their aftermath, during which we see a good deal of self-sacrifice, caring about others, and heroism. It is a relevant concept when discussing mothers who have lost children. Altruism refers to giving up direct gratification of needs in favor of fulfilling the needs of others with vicarious satisfaction gained through identification with the other, a significant aspect of mothering. It appears to continue in maternal bereavement. Members of Compassionate Friends ranked altruistic experiences as one of the most helpful in their membership with that group. The parents said such events helped in "feeling worthwhile" and "helping others lessens my pain."[31] Non-group members also noted altruistic activity as gratifying to them.

The final coping mechanism to be discussed is projection, where feelings that cannot be tolerated in oneself are attributed to others. In cases of loss through death or separation, anger or blame may be projected on to others who pose a threat to the mother. Projection is closely tied into events of loss in general which stimulate feelings of guilt, shame, helplessness, and longing in addition to anger. These are difficult emotions to tolerate, perhaps even more so when they surface with regard to the loss of a child. Placing responsibility for the loss on other people or institutions acts to minimize guilt and helplessness and legitimize any displaced feelings, particularly anger. It further serves to perpetuate an illusion of control. The experience of loss continually reminds us that life is uncertain. If responsibility for death, separation, loss of a job, dream, health, and so on can be established in the external world, then someone is in control at a time when the mourner is feeling helpless.

We all strive to make sense of our experiences. The intrapsychic coping mechanisms discussed here have been those primarily associated with, and expected in, mourning. Individuals differ as to what degree they utilize these defenses, contributing to personalized coping styles.

Psychological defense is just one factor that influences mourning and makes each experience of bereavement unique. Additional variables, such as the personalities, history, and special relationship between mother and child are explored in Chapter Three, the context and circumstances of the loss in Chapter Four, and social relationships that support or inhibit the mourning process in Chapters Seven and Eight, also play essential roles in understanding the course of mourning.

NOTES

1. George Pollock, "Mourning and Adaptation," *International Journal of Psychoanalysis, 42* (1961): 341-361. Pollock integrates physiological principles with psychological theory to describe the intrapsychic dynamics of the mourning process.

2. Sigmund Freud, "Mourning and Melancholia," (1917) in *Sigmund Freud: Collected Papers,* ed. E. Jones (New York: Basic Books, 1959).

3. George Pollock, "Process and Affect: Mourning and Grief," *International Journal of Psychoanalysis, 59* (1978): 255-276. Pollock contends that mourning is a universal adaptational and transformational process, phylogenetically evolved and present as a reaction to loss, but not solely to object loss or death.

4. Arthur Carr, "Bereavement as a Relative Experience," in *Bereavement: Its Psychosocial Aspects,* ed. B. Schoenberg et al. (New York: Columbia University Press, 1975).

5. Robert W. White, "Strategies of Adaptation: An Attempt at Systematic Description," in *Human Adaptation: Coping with Life Crises,* ed. R. Moos (Lexington, MA: Heath, 1976).

6. Marc Fried, "Grieving for a Lost Home," in *The Environment of the Metropolis,* ed. L.J. Duhl (New York: Basic Books, 1962); Irving Janis, *Psychological Stress* (New York: John Wiley and Sons, 1958). Janis studied surgical patients' coping patterns; Colin Murray Parkes, *Bereavement: Studies of Grief in Adult Life* (New York: International Universities Press, 1972). Parkes compares the stages of adjustment in amputation with death of a loved one, and discusses the experience of "loss of self" and "psychological mutilation"; Kai Erikson, *Everything in Its Path* (New York: Simon and Schuster, 1976), is a moving account of the aftermath of floods in West Virginia; Robert J. Lifton, *The Broken Connection: On Death and the Continuity of Life* (New York: Simon and Schuster, 1979); Martha Wolfenstein, *Disaster: A Psychological Essay* (Glencoe, IL: The Free Press, 1957); Patricia Frieberg and Margaret Bridwell, "An Intervention Model for Rape and Unwanted Pregnancy," *Counseling Psychologist, 6* (1976): 50-53; May Romm, "Loss of Sexual Function in the Female," in *Loss and Grief: Psychological Management in Medical Practice,* ed. B. Schoenberg, A. Carr, D. Peretz, and A. Kutscher (New York: Columbia University Press, 1970), 178-188.

7. George Pollock, "Process and Affect"; Arthur Carr, "Bereavement as a Relative Experience."

8. For discussions of the mourning inherent in adolescence, see Wolfenstein and Freud. Martha Wolfenstein, "How Is a Mourning Possible?" *Psychoanalytic Study of the Child, 21* (1966): 93-123; Anna Freud, "Adolescence," *Psychoanalytic Study of the Child, 13* (1958): 255-278; Roger Gould, *Transformations* (New York: Simon and Schuster, 1978); George Pollock, "Process and Affect." Gould and Pollock explain how life transitions and aging also induce mourning.

9. David Peretz, "Development, Object-Relationships and Loss," in *Loss and Grief: Psychological Management in Medical Practice,* ed. B. Schoenberg, A. Carr, D. Peretz, and A. Kutscher (New York: Columbia University Press, 1970).

10. Ira Glick, Robert Weiss, and Colin Murray Parkes, *The First Year of Bereavement* (New York: John Wiley and Sons, 1974); George Pollock, "Mourning and Adaptation," Colin Murray Parkes, "The First Year of Bereavement: A Longitudinal Study of the Reactions of London Widows to the Death of Their Husbands," *Psychiatry, 33* (1970): 444-467; Colin Murray Parkes, *Bereavement: Studies of Grief;* Colin Murray Parkes, "Unexpected and Untimely Bereavement: A Statistical Study of Young Boston Widows and Widowers," in *Bereavement: Its Psychosocial Aspects,* ed. B. Schoenberg et al. (New York: Columbia University Press, 1975): 119-138.

11. Ira Glick, Robert Weiss, and Colin Murray Parkes, *The First Year;* Colin Murray Parkes, "The First Year of Bereavement," *Bereavement: Studies of Grief;* "Unexpected and Untimely Bereavement"; R. Ramsay and J. Happee, "The Stress of Bereavement: Components and Treatment," in *Stress and Anxiety,* Vol.1, ed. L. Sarason (London: John Wiley and Sons, 1977).

12. George Pollock, "Process and Affect"; David Peretz, "Reaction to Loss."

13. Kai Erikson, *Everything in Its Path;* Louis Degner, "Death in Disaster: Implications for Bereavement," *Essence, 1* (2976): 69-77; Erich Lindemann, "Symptomatology and Management of Acute Grief," *American Journal of Psychiatry, 101* (1944): 141-148.

14. George Pollock, "Mourning and Adaptation."

15. Kai Erikson, *Everything in Its Path.*

16. Colin Murray Parkes, *Bereavement: Studies of Grief.*

17. Ibid.

18. George Pollock, "Mourning and Adaptation."

19. David Peretz, "Reaction to Loss"; Erich Lindemann describes "distortions" of normal grief in "Symptomatology and Management of Acute Grief."

20. Helen Deutsch, "Absence of Grief," *Psychoanalytic Quarterly, 6* (1937): 12-22; Sigmund Freud, "Mourning and Melancholia"; George Engel, *Psychological Development in Health and Disease* (Philadelphia: W.B. Saunders, 1962).

21. Joseph Smith, "Identificatory Styles in Depression and Grief," *International Journal of Psychoanalysis, 52* (1971): 259-266.

22. Robert J. Lifton, *The Broken Connection,* p. 189.

23. George Engel and A. Schmale have written extensively on psychosomatic illness. For example, see: George Engel, *Psychological Development,* "A Life Setting Conducive to Illness," *Bulletin of the Menninger, 32* (1968): 355-365; George Engel and A. Schmale, "Psychoanalytic Theory of Somatic Disorder," *Journal of the American Psychoanalytic Association, 15* (1967): 344-363; A. Schmale, "Giving Up as a Final Common Pathway to Changes in Health," *Advances in Psychosomatic Medicine, 8* (1972): 20-40; A. Schmale and George Engel, "The Giving Up-Given Up Complex," *Archives of General Psychiatry, 17* (1967): 135-145.

24. For examples of extreme bereavement reactions see: Marcia Kraft Goin, R.W. Burgoyne, and John Goin, "Timeless Attachment to a Dead Relative," *American Journal of Psychiatry, 136* no.7 (1979): 988-989. They describe normal but intense attachments to dead spouses; Mardi J. Horowitz, Nancy Wilner, Charles Marmar, and Janice Krupnick, "Pathological Grief and the Activation of Latent Self-Images," *American Journal of Psychiatry, 137* no.10 (1980): 1157-1162. They present observations of cases where pathology resulted from emerging negative self-images, previously held in check by the deceased, that prevent the normal course of mourning; George Pollock, "Manifestations of Abnormal Mourning: Homicide and Suicide Following the Death of Another," *The Annual of Psychoanalysis,* Vol.4 (1976): 225-249. He presents suicides and homicides as anniversary reactions to the death of another, theorizing that underlying these acts are wishes to reunite with the deceased.

25. Robert J. Lifton, *The Broken Connection.*

26. Sigmund Freud, "Mourning and Melancholia"; George Krupp, "The Bereavement Reaction," *Psychoanalytic Study of Society,* Vol.2 (New York: International Universities Press, 1962): 42-74; George Pollock, "On Mourning and Anniversaries: The Relationship of Culturally Constituted Defensive Systems to Intrapsychic Adaptive Processes," *Israel Annals of Psychiatry, 10.* no.1 (1972): 3-19; Hans Loewald, "Internalization, Separation, Mourning and the Superego," *Psychoanalytic Quarterly, 31* (1962): 483-504; Karl Abraham, "Object-loss and Introjection in Normal Mourning and in Abnormal States of Mind," in *Selected Papers of Karl Abraham* (New York: Basic Books, 1927, originally published, 1924), 433-443. The dissenting view about identification is expressed by Parkes, *Bereavement: Studies of Grief.*

27. Sigmund Freud, "Mourning and Melancholia," p. 154.

28. Sigmund Freud, "The Ego and the Id," *Standard Edition, 19* (London: Hogarth Press, 1961, originally published, 1923): 3-68.

29. Hans Loewald, "Internalization, Separation"; J. Smith, "Identificatory Styles."

30. Roy Schafer, "The Fates of the Immortal Objects," in *Aspects of Internalization* (New York: International Universities Press, 1968).

31. Morton Lieberman, Lawrence Borman and Associates, *Self-Help Groups for Coping with Crisis* (San Francisco: Jossey-Bass, 1979).

three

The Mother/Child Relationship

The death of a child is an event that occurs in the mother's inner and outer worlds. Both are real and must be understood. This chapter concentrates on the internal world of thought and feelings a mother has for her child. It is in this world that the unique meaning of that relationship gains clarity. It gives us insights into the meanings of the subsequent loss and reactions to the death.

The meaning is sought through an understanding of motherhood, then, more specifically, the meaning of that particular child, keeping in mind the complex variables at work—personality, gender, circumstance, and history of the mother and child, both as inbdividuals and together, all occurring in a specific context and period of development. It is far afield of this work to do justice to all these influences, but in acknowledging them we can begin to understand all that is lost when a child dies.

THE SPECIAL RELATIONSHIP

> I probably relied on him pretty heavily as a friend.
>
> (Thelma)

> She wasn't an easy kid to raise . . . but she was extremely stubborn and strong-willed. That's what made her an achiever.
>
> (Sherry)

I really shouldn't call him my favorite child, but he was.

(Jane)

For most women, motherhood represents an intense personal investment, and psychoanalytic writers generally agree that maternal feelings have their roots in childhood. The relationship of a mother and child has grown, in good measure, from the mother's own development. Two aspects of her development that are related to motivations for motherhood are: the reproductive drive, which is expressed in the adult tendency to give and aid in times of distress; and the lingering receptive tendencies from her own childhood that facilitate identification with her child.

Other views put less stress on biological aspects, drives, and identification and more on gender and sex-role socialization concluding that mothering is reproduced through generations in women's personality structures by their mothers.[1] In either view, it is easy to see the deep roots of mothering and how the woman's development, including learning and identification with her own mother and mother figures, shapes her attitudes toward motherhood and determines some of her behavior toward her own children.

Freud commented on the narcissistic goals and satisfactions in parenthood:

> The child shall have a better time than his parents; he shall not be subject to the necessities which they have recognized as paramount in life. Illness, death, renunciation of enjoyment, restrictions on his own will, shall not touch him; the laws of nature and of society shall be abrogated in his favour; he shall once more really be the centre and core of creation—"His Majesty the Baby," as we once fancied ourselves. The child shall fulfill those wishful dreams of the parents which they never carried out—the boy shall become a great man and a hero in his father's place, and the girl shall marry a prince as a tardy compensation for her mother. At the most touchy point in the narcissistic system, the immortality of the ego, which is so hard pressed by reality, security is achieved by taking refuge in the child. Parental love, which is so moving and at bottom so childish, is nothing but the parents' narcissism born again, which, transformed into object-love, unmistakably reveals its former nature.[2]

More recently, the motivations that give rise to disturbances in the child or in the dyad have been examined. The ulterior motives in mothering can be: the desire to please or punish the husband; the use as a pawn in marital conflict; to keep the marriage together; to win approval of other people; to fulfill the stereotyped ideal of family life; to deny anxiety with regard to frigidity and sterility; to make the child into a parent figure; to use the child as a symbol of suffering; to mold the child into a more perfect edition of one's self; and, finally, the urge to give the child what the mother herself never had.[3]

This list is by no means complete and concentrates on the problematic aspects, but these two summaries do give some idea of the complexity in wanting a child and the multiple meanings that any child can have during its lifetime for the mother.

Another powerful motivation to mother is the accomplishment of one's girlhood ideal of becoming a giving, good, even "perfect" mother. It is the maternal ideal to place the child's interests before her own. If carried to masochistic extremes, it can be pathological, but in the normal relationship there is a pleasure in the child's care. Ordinary mothering is an example of sublimated ideals, commitment, love, and the ability to nurture. Having ideals and the ability to live up to them, to some extent, is necessary for motherliness.

The ideal mother has no interests of her own. But just as the mother gratifies the child, so the child gratifies the mother. And just as the child does not recognize the mother as having a separate identity, the mother often sees the child as a part of herself whose interests match her own. She is the caretaker but is also identified with the child. Through the gratifying experiences of being a mother the woman gains confidence in her motherliness and approaches the realization of one ideal: to be a good mother. She gains from the health and development of her child, in the process resolving or reconciling some of her conflicts with her own mother, gaining in her own development and enriching the evolving relationship with her child.[4]

In a recent study of the first pregnancy in a sample of middle-class women, it was found that they regarded children as a basic part of the meaning of life and essential to their view of themselves as women. Simply having had the child enhanced the woman's self-esteem.[5]

The psychological symbiosis of pregnancy decreases gradually with the child's birth, growth, and development. Even when there is a greater physical distance between the two, with increased separation and individuation, the "living or 'feeling together' of two human beings in close union for their mutual benefit can still be designated a symbiotic type of relationship."[6] This symbiotic relationship, or what Balint called "instinctive maternity," with mother and child sharing an identity, can be contrasted with "civilized maternity," which is the more mature capacity for loving in a social sense that is grounded in external reality.[7] It raises the question of whether, or to what degree, the residue of "instinctive maternity" persists in even the generally healthy relationships between mothers and their children. Certainly mother and child remain, for a long time, in a reciprocal if not symbiotic relationship, one gratifying to both.

As the tasks of parenthood are completed successfully, resulting in promoting the child's growth, the mother undergoes changes. Each maturational phase completed in the child sees a concomitant development in the mother as a person who has had to work through issues of her own. The working-through facilitates her ability to let go of the child as he or she was and adapt to the next phase of the relationship.

Mothering requires ever-changing adjustments and coordinations toward successful resolutions of each of the challenges and conflicts posed in the rearing of an ever-changing child. The "function of interaction," one concept proposed by Gut to explain bereavement intensity, refers to the sum total of purposes served mutually by the two. A second concept, the "scope of the interaction," refers to how great or limited a number and variety of behavior patterns, including thoughts and feelings; how large a range of the mourner's personal potentials have been engaged; and, in general, how much of the mourner's sense of identity, meaning, and purpose of life and responsibility have been involved. The more of the self that has been engaged, the more devastating the loss and the more demanding the task of readaptation.[8]

Others also note the deprivation after a loss that robs the survivor of those essential "supplies" that were previously provided. What is it, then, that a child "supplies" to its mother? Certainly, each dyad is unique, the interaction being different between that mother and that child than between any other pair. The loss of that child means the loss of that unique relationship. A daughter may carry a different meaning than a son, an older child differs from a younger one, a sickly or troublesome child provides conflicts and gratifications that an easy or healthy child does not. A child with whom the mother identifies has a meaning that is different from one whom she identifies with another individual. Whatever the complex meaning of that child, the relationship is severed upon death.

If the child is necessary in the mother's achievement of being the good mother, the mother has been cheated of an important part of herself. The mother has made earlier costly adjustments to motherhood and may have renounced some of her other potentials or inclinations to facilitate this relationship. Upon the loss of the child, the depth of this adjustment works against her. "Doors have been closed, bridges have been burnt."[9] Readjustment takes time, energy, and effort. It includes idealization in an effort to hold on to the satisfactions that are gone in an effort to remind one's self that the lost relationship *has* been worth the price of the adjustment, the pain of the loss, and the necessary readjustment.

The adjustments that a woman makes to motherhood, beginning with pregnancy and continuing endlessly throughout the span of mothering, affects a major portion of her life and decisions. The past is gone, and with the death of the child, some of the future is also gone. Any confrontation with death means not only the loss of a loved one, but an assault on her sense of immortality. Given that a child is the major link to the future, it may be all the more devastating.

Certainly, looking at the normative interaction of mothers in their middle years and children in adolescence or late adolescence, we expect to see issues of separation and individuation. But they are also women who, under better circumstances, are beginning to enjoy new rewards. Many women enjoy their freedom, their husbands, and their grown children more than ever before. The mother sees her child's emerging identity, for better or worse, and faces a period of more relaxed vigilance than previously.

The mother in the middle years has her own developmental issues to address. She must accept the fact that youth and childhood are gone. This involves physical changes in her body. With this understanding is the acknowledgment of mortality, involving limited time ahead in which to live and to accomplish all that she intends. She faces the loss of childbearing functions, even if no children were born, and adjusts to a different relationship with children who are growing up. Her parents are aging or dead, necessitating additional changes in her status as a daughter. The final task is a more mature acceptance of the responsibility for her own life, relinquishing the illusions of male perfection. Aspects of personality that may have been suppressed until this time can be integrated into her personality structure. In these tasks there are losses that she mourns, and also the realization that there are gains in middle adulthood that were unavailable at earlier times. There is an intersection of her own mortality with that of her child.[10] The death of a child screams "failure" to a woman who has devoted herself to that task.

If these are some of the dynamics of mothering and the developmental tasks of women in the middle years, how do they translate in specific instances to real women and their children? In the relationship between Louise and her son Larry, the interaction of the mother's personality and history with that of the child's personality and past is vividly shown.

Louise is an attractive and warm 43-year-old Roman Catholic woman. She has had some college and works as a secretary in a small neighborhood company, a job that provides some satisfaction but is not as personally rewarding as the role of mother. Her son, Larry, was the second of four children and the older of the two boys. At age 18, he and two of his friends were killed instantly in a head-on auto crash. Louise was open and articulate about the intense grief she has been experiencing, and relates it to the specialness of this son:

> Mind if I go back a few years? When Larry was 13 years old he told me one day that he had a bad problem, that he was having leg trouble. He had lived with us for 13 years and nobody noticed it . . . . It turned out to be that he had a massive growth. Yet living with him, we didn't realize it . . . . The doctor took X-rays. Nothing showed . . . . So he put him in a cast for six weeks . . . . Still nothing showed up on the X-rays, but he wasn't any better.

After more tests and exploratory surgery, they found the growth and told the family he had two years to live.

> When they came out of surgery and told us that he was going to die from cancer . . . (it) was identical to the feeling I had when they came through the door and told me he was killed . . . . We prayed. The whole town prayed. Everybody we knew prayed.

Days later the doctors decided to try a delicate operation. It lasted many hours, and for the three months that followed, they waited to see if he would ever walk or grow normally:

> He came out of it just perfect. He walked, he grew, he was intelligent. As a 13-year-old boy, he grew up a whole lot at that time. He was just a very special kid. He knew God. We brought him back. This time it was like God is not going to give me a chance this time to keep him. I thought that he had come back to us for a reason, and I guess maybe he did. We had five years . . . but yet, to lose him again

> . . . to have him killed so fast and so suddenly . . . I guess he was a miracle if you want to believe in miracles.

Larry had grown up into a young man whom his mother liked, "a super kid" who fit into the life of college and the family. Louise appreciated his character, which matched her own in religious outlook and caring for others.

There was some of Larry's specialness. He had a personality that she valued, he matured as a result of his illness, and, very significantly, they shared a past that included a severe crisis in which she believed she had helped pull him through. She had been successful as a protective and caring mother during the hospitalization and recovery period.

Louise, more than any other woman in the study, articulated the helplessness of being unable to protect her son from death and the intense desire to have been able to do something for him, a conflict that was still experienced almost two years later, and the primary struggle in her bereavement.

In the relationship between Anne and her daughter there is a different kind of specialness. This shows the interaction of personalities in an intense and ambivalent relationship. It is not intended to portray the norm, but rather to highlight a mother's identification with her daughter at a particular stage in both their lives.

Anne, 44, has an antique shop and an appreciation for fine things. Her marriage has not been a happy one, and she has invested a great deal of time and energy in her two sons and daughter. The oldest of the three, Anni, her namesake, was 19 when she was killed in a particularly mutilating auto accident:

> I think it is more intense for a mother and daughter. We went round and round. I loved her dearly, but I didn't particularly like her, not at that stage. She was a very beautiful girl, extremely beautiful. This is one reason, I think, (that) killed her, it went to her head. She was very selfish and self-centered, entranced with her own beauty. We spoiled her horribly.
>
> . . . The rules didn't apply to her. She could do or say just about anything and get away with it because boys spoiled her . . . . She would have outgrown it. She would have turned into a really great person, but she got stopped midstream.

About her daughter's personality she said, "She could be so persuasive, you know, she wanted her own way . . . ."

Contrast that with her statement about herself:

> I have a way of making things work for me. If I want something, I get it, and I want beautiful things . . . I am very single-minded. When I went to college, I got a 4.0. It got me an ulcer, but when I chose to do something, I do it all stops pulled.

They shared a passion for collecting antique glass and both loved attending shows and sales together. About their shared interest Anne said,

> It's a funny thing. What was my greatest love is now my greatest pain . . . . It was all for her. And it wasn't for her selflessly, it was for her selfishly. The kick I got out of getting it for her was my joy . . . . Even though I'd find it, I gave it to her 'cause it meant nothing, and she'd go "woooo" you know, and off she'd go.

Anni's death triggered attacks of hyperventilation during which Anne believed she was dying. She became intensely despairing and suicidal, resulting in part from the special identification between Anne and her daughter. Anne's struggle, at the time of the interview, was to find a reason that would make living worthwhile without her daughter.

> My life is over . . . . I was one of those poor slobs that was other directed. I never lived for myself, I lived for my children . . . . Right or wrong. When I lost her, she was my direction in life . . . . My problem now is suicide, probably . . . . You can't treasure life because then you have to acknowledge how much you've lost.

Relationships with children are not static but dynamic and changing over time. A death at one time of life may have a different meaning than at another, but object loss, by its very definition, means that the person was of significance and value to the bereaved.

The relationship of Deborah with her daughter shows the importance of the mother's stage of development in the meaning of the loss. It is more usual to think about the child as growing and changing than the mothers, but adulthood has its own stages. These mothers were in their middle years, a special time of life with its own problems and rewards. The losses of Deborah highlight some of the issues for midlife mothers.

Deborah, 47, and her daughter Dee, 9, the youngest child in the study, had a different kind of specialness. Deborah had raised three children who were out of the house. Dee was the late child, the one born into an affluent household where both parents had time, money, and attention to lavish exclusively on her. They also had grown children who were willing babysitters so they enjoyed the freedom to travel and go out. Deborah was a college graduate who had gone back to school for a Master's degree in advertising and worked part-time, occasionally finding a job for her young daughter in a commercial. The place that Dee occupied in her mother's life was strongly related to the timing and circumstances of her birth, and the shared enjoyment of Deborah's talent and work. Deborah also relished the ties to younger women and school activities that Dee provided, relinking her to a world she enjoyed. When Dee was killed by a car, Deborah lost her child, the role of mother, the younger friends, and the desire to continue with a career so tied to her daughter:

> One day, you know, there I was, suburban matron with a fourth grader, you know, going to Brownie meetings, all that stuff, playing tennis with those women, you know, being asked to bring the treat and car pooling, and the next minute that child was gone. My common bond with those women was gone, and a few months later I was a grandmother.

Deborah was at a stage that bridged two worlds, the final child at home was the last link to active mothering. Without her, it was gone.

> I enjoyed all that so much, more than most of those mothers . . . . and I had this chance to say, "Oh, you know, it doesn't last very long."

Dee had multiple meanings for her mother: the last child, youth, and work. Deborah lost a great deal, and her struggle during mourning was to adapt to the losses that seemed to permeate every aspect of her life.

One more dyad will be looked at: this time in order to see the influence of conflict on the meaning of the loss to the mother. Lydia is a vibrant, expressive woman. At 39, she was separated from her husband, living alone nearby, and heavily invested in a graduate school nursing program. Her two teenage children lived with their father. Lydia had a long history of conflict with her 16-year-old daughter, and part of her time in therapy was spent trying to resolve some of those difficulties. The girl had been running away for several years, so once when Lydia could not find her, she went out looking. When she entered the home she had shared with the family, she found her daughter dead from an overdose of drugs and alcohol:

> The meaninglessness of the loss of that life is hard and it upset my whole sense of being able to ultimately work things through with people that I care for. You know, my belief had been that we can work it out. There's no longer, we can no longer do that . . . . She made a clear statement . . . . that she doesn't believe that it's possible to work things out.

The hopes she had for herself and the child were destroyed. She had to face the loss of her only daughter and the additional painful realization that there was no longer any hope of resolving the problems.

> Shortly after her death, or immediately after her death and for, I don't know, a long period of time, like months, there was a persistent visual image of her, and what I kept hearing over and over again was, "I didn't do it on purpose, Ma, I didn't do it on purpose, Ma." . . . and I don't know if that's just my hope . . . .

This situation also shows the additional stresses, some of which had nothing to do with the death: marital problems, career demands, previous behavior problems, money worries. A mother is not spared the ordinary problems of living just because the child has died. The other stresses often become insignificant, at least temporarily, as this crisis preempts time and energy. All that a woman brings to motherhood is based on her past and present life, influenced also by the child's uniqueness and situational factors.

In this chapter so far, the attempt has been made to examine the complex meaning of the child in order to understand the loss for the mother. With this knowledge we can ask the question, "What has been lost?"

WHAT HAS BEEN LOST?

> '(I said) somehow I didn't do a good enough job,' and they said that 'You did the best you could,' I said, 'But it wasn't good enough.'

> They said, 'You don't understand, you did the best you could.' And that is what's so hard to accept.
>
> (Lydia)

Multiple levels of loss occur with the death. This study indicates three major and interrelated types of loss: (1) the loss of a loved child as an aspect of one's self; (2) the loss of future hopes and expectations; and (3) the confrontation with false illusions as a result of the death.

The Loss As an Aspect of One's Self

The loss of a child as an aspect of one's self relates to a basic assumption that motherhood is far more than a series of functions performed. We have proposed "motherliness" as a central aspect of female personality development, related to identification with one's own mother, biological functioning, and personality. Losing a child, even when others remain in the family, assaults basic aspects of a woman's identity. Sandy unknowingly paraphrased Freud's 1914 statement on the narcissistic goals of parenthood:

> A lot of it is very selfish really . . . . The selfishness is not having him. I think a lot of times, oh, I'm not being selfish, I'm thinking of him, of what he's missing. But it is selfish because you want to see him do them. That's what you live for. Raising kids all those years, screaming and yelling and having a nervous breakdown. You live for the day when you can sit back and see a decent human being that's enjoying life and having a good time and bringing happiness to others. That's your fulfillment.

These women were unable to guide their children into adulthood and unable to protect them from dying prematurely. The failure results in lowered self-esteem because they blame themselves for all they did not do. They feel useless and regretful. Deborah noted that she was sorry for the times she disciplined the child, spent time away from her, and acted in normal mothering ways. She realized that she had to do those things, but it had been future-oriented, raising her child into adulthood. Much of the mother/child relationship is based on the premise that there is a future and actions taken in the present have later rewards.

Mothering is an example of sublimated ideals: the satisfaction is altruistic, indirect, coming through the development of the child. The mother takes care of, but also identifies with, the child, thereby gaining from the child's progress. When the child is lost, some aspects of the mother's identity are lost, too. Loss of any person close is loss of self.

The Loss of Future Hopes and Expectations

The second type of loss was one of future hopes and expectations. Surprisingly, the women had similar basic hopes whether the child was male or female, although Marion noted that with a girl's death, "You're losing more of your own future." Anne commented on the closer relationship possible with a daughter than a son.

Eight of the women interviewed had lost daughters and eight had lost sons. The mothers of girls more often noted similarities with the daughter in personality, interests, and career goals, although two mothers of sons identified with their personalities. The daughters appear to have had closer relationships to the mother and were perceived as tied more directly to the mother's future and hopes, but women often mentioned identical expectations for sons and daughters. Specifically these included seeing the child get married, have a career, and raise a family. More generally, the loss, as expressed by Louise, was

> He was just doing . . . and he was so enthused . . . but I never got to see what he could have done with his life . . . . It stopped before we were able to find out what he was really able to accomplish with his life.

Several of them mused about having another year, a little longer, grandchildren; maybe then it would have been easier.

> Sometimes I think that he would have graduated from college and he would have had a job for some years and I would have known what he was going to do. Maybe it wouldn't have been so hard. But it would have been hard. Then there would have been another reason why.
>
> (Louise)

There could not be a "right" time.

There were two major differences in the hopes expressed. The first was related to the age of the child, and the second to whether or not the relationship was conflictual. Surprisingly, there was no clear significance found that primarily related to the birth order of the child. The women who lost children in late adolescence or early adulthood, most of whom still lived at home, were mourning the "things he won't get to do." The mothers of the younger children did not yet see a clear future path for the child. They mourned the loss of continuing years of nurturing, companionship, and the daily tasks of mothering still needed by those children.

As was seen earlier in examining the specialness of the children, some relationships were far more conflictual than others. For the mothers who had good relationships with the child and whose children were proudly launched, they missed being able to see their potential. The mothers who had problematic relationships with their child experienced a double loss: that of not resolving the problems, in addition to losing the hopes that he or she would ultimately turn out well.

There were also two instances where the child had recently come through a difficult period and hopes were high. Betty's son had been hyperactive and on medication for years, and it wasn't until two years before his death that he had matured and settled down, giving up previously violent behavior. Frances's daughter had died only six months after her own husband's death. This was a double loss. The mother had gotten her through a bad time and was beginning to have positive and realistic hopes for the future.

Successfully completed tasks of parenthood also promote growth in the parent. When the child dies, the mourning for him or her is for all the things that the child will miss, but the mother mourns the fact that she, too, was "stopped mid-stream."

> . . . I didn't get to somehow launch that child, whatever all that involved, so I'm left with a lot of unfinished business, too.
>
> (Lydia)

Because mothering is such a central part of their identities, even for those with careers, there is an ongoing frustration at being unable to complete the task with this child. Throughout the struggle of adapting to the loss, and often in the later stages of reorganizing their lives, we will see the attempts to complete the jobs of motherhood or what has been called the symbolic search for repair.[11] These women are not planning to "start over," either with children or work.

Most of the women acknowledged fantasies of having another child after the death of their son or daughter. All but Lydia have disregarded the idea because of age, physical inability, or fear that it would prove to be a disastrous attempt at replacement. But in looking at the questionnaires, 33 (26 percent) of the women who responded had children after the death of the child and five more were pregnant. These were the younger women, not those in the middle years, and most of them (29) had lost a child under the age of three. Chodoff et al. found that five out of 24 mothers became pregnant during or immediately after a child's fatal illness and two others were trying to conceive or adopt. They suggest that these were restitutive efforts that were accompanying the detachment from the dying or dead child.[12] For these women, in their middle years, there was no starting over, distinguishing this time of life.

Most research on the developmental tasks of the middle years assumes the confrontation with mortality to be a major dynamic. In conjunction with facing "time left to live," the woman grapples with giving up childbearing abilities and functions, illusions of youth, protection, and work. This group of women was assaulted by these issues, but their confrontation with death appears to have left them less fearful of dying than before the loss. It might be expected that the women in the first year of mourning would identify with death, the wish to die, hopes for reunion, and escape from the pain of the loss, thereby temporarily putting their own fear of death aside, but the pattern continued among women in all stages of mourning. They said that they "don't think about death," "refuse to worry," or "don't fear it." Most quickly add that they are not ready to die now, but with an acceptance of the child's death, there seems to be a greater acceptance of their own mortality. The most common explanation was that facing the loss is a harder task than facing their own death. They fear losing someone else more than dying themselves and, for those who believe in an afterlife, they are certain that the life of the survivor is the more difficult road.

It appears that coping with the death of a child tends to overshadow conscious tasks of reassessment in the middle years. The focus is on adapting to this major change and any existential issues of midlife are struggled with in the context and parameters of this loss.

The Loss of Illusions

The illusions that were shattered as a result of the child's death are existential in nature, resulting from the death itself or the coping involved in the mourning process. Central losses of this type are: the illusions of security and protection from tragedy; the illusion that there is fairness in or control over death; and the illusion that there are answers to questions such as, "Why my child?"

The comforting belief that bad things happen to *other* people was abruptly shattered. Louise said,

> This was really the first death that I was really involved with. I mean, I was able to handle everything in my life up until this time . . . I didn't realize what kind of complications and how rough it really gets by losing a son.

There is no preparation for handling the death of a child. The women felt their sense of efficacy shattered by the event. No one could protect any of the women from the intense emotions of mourning, and no one could do the work of mourning for them. Others can help, and they do, but the intensity of the grief was an intimate and isolating experience, shared only within certain limits, depending on personality and relationships. The woman's sense of security is threatened. The foundation on which she has built aspects of identity and relies on for much of her daily functioning is changed.

The second illusion, that of some order or fairness in life and death, must be confronted. Anne said that it didn't matter that she had been good and done all the right things in life. It was frightening to think

> There aren't any rules. There is no justice. There is no fair . . . I grew up with Walt Disney.

The loss of a child, perhaps more than other deaths, causes a sense of "wrongness" in the order of things. The mother is robbed of the expectation that children should and will outlive their parents, and that the time, adjustments, and investments made in a child will assure his or her future.

There is rarely a "right" time for anyone to die, and certainly not a child. Feifel discusses the fact that important people in our lives have differential life expectancies. We assume, and if asked could probably articulate, the order in which death was expected to claim people who have meaning to us. He refers to it as the "pecking order of death." The implications for this "rightness" in the order of dying go beyond the variable of age, but it provides a good example. There is an inherent sense of "rightness" that if people we love must die, then it is more justified that the oldest die first. It touches people's basic hope of "fair play" and an orderliness to life and death. "The fact that Death calls the 'first in line' shows that It is playing the game fairly, faithful to the unwritten rules. The death of an old person can help to support the survivor's belief that a kind of rationality prevails. One's own turn will not be coming up for a while."[13] The death of a child goes counter to the rules about death.

Another dimension to shattered illusions, unexplored in most previous studies of bereavement, is supportive of Freud's observation that an object's transience seems to decrease its worth.[14] Having a child in this society carries with it the expectation that he or she will outlive the parent. Although mothers expect the relationship to change, and to give up the child in many ways, the child's survival beyond her life is a strong belief and expectation. There is no previous experience, either real or imagined, that prepares the mother for this loss. The illusions of orderliness, fairness, control, protection, and future are shattered.

Also, our society has increased our unfamiliarity with death. Technology, medicine, and the advancements of our century have allowed people to live longer now than they have ever lived before. More people have both children and parents alive than ever in history. It was not always so. Other times and other cultures accepted the fact that some, if not all, of their children would die before reaching adulthood. The advances in prolonging life have created psychological drawbacks.

The third illusion is that there are reasons and answers for things that happen in this world. The women divided on this issue: some found answers, others did not.

For several, the bizarreness of the accident or some circumstance about it only reinforced the belief that it was meant to be: We are part of a grand plan. Sylvia recalled that her daughter was killed by a flying piece of metal that hit no one else at the bus stop. Mandy's son was the only one killed out of the four boys in the truck. "To me that says it all, you know, that it was meant to be and it was his time." Sherry noted that the girls on one side of the bus were killed and those on the other side lived. The examples go on and on, and each helps prove to someone who needs to believe that there was an answer. Even if the reason cannot be known, there must be one. Some of the women were comforted; others struggled with accepting the existence of a reason they did not know. Still others said there was no reason and they were left to accept a world that was sometimes random and dangerous.

The examination of these components of loss in the child's death leads to the formulation that an event of this magnitude captures the mourner and engages all coping resources to adapt to the loss. The intrapsychic and behavioral strategies begin immediately and continue for years.

NOTES

1. Nancy Chodorow, *The Reproduction of Mothering: Psychoanalysis and the Sociology of Gender* (Berkeley: University of California Press, 1978).

2. Sigmund Freud, "On Narcissism," *Standard Edition, 14* (1957, originally published 1914), p. 91.

3. Nathan Ackerman, "Disturbances of Mothering and Criteria for Treatment," *American Journal of Orthopsychiatry, 26,* no.2 (1956): 252-263.

4. Alice Balint, "Love for the Mother and Mother-Love," in *Primary Love and Psychoanalytic Technique,* ed. M. Balint (London: Hogarth Press, 1952, originally published, 1939); Therese Benedek, "Parenthood as a Developmental Phase," *Journal of the American Psychological Association, 7,* no.3 (1959): 389-417; Harold Blum, "The Maternal Ego Ideal and the Regulation of Maternal Qualities," in *The Course of Life: Psychoanalytic Contributions Toward Understanding Personality Development,* Vol.3, ed. S. Greenspan and G. Pollock (Washington, D.C.: U.S. Department of Health and Human Services, U.S. Government Printing Office, 1981).

5. Myra Liefer, *Psychological Effects of Motherhood: A Study of First Pregnancy* (New York: Praeger, 1980).

6. George Pollock, "On Symbiosis and Symbiotic Neurosis," *International Journal of Psychoanalysis, 45* (1964): 1-30.

7. Alice Balint, "Love for the Mother."

8. Emmy Gut, "Some Aspects of Adult Mourning," *Omega, 5* (1974): 323-340.

9. Ibid., p. 344.

10. The developmental tasks of a woman's middle years are addressed by different writers. For example, relinquishing youth and accepting mortality, see Eliot Jaques, "Death and the Mid-life Crisis," *International Journal of Psychoanalysis, 46* (1965): 502-514; Otto Kernberg, *Internal World and External Reality* (New York: Jason Aronson, 1980). Loss of childbearing functions is referred to by Lillian B. Rubin, *Women of a Certain Age* (New York: Harper & Row, 1979); Pauline Bart, "Depression in Middle-

Age Women," in *Women in Sexist Society,* ed. V. Gornick (New York: Basic Books, 1971); Bernice Neugarten and Nancy Datan, "The Midlife Years," in *American Handbook of Psychiatry,* Vol. 1, 2nd ed., ed. S. Arieti (New York: Basic Books, 1974). Taking responsibility for one's life is discussed by Lillian B. Rubin, *Women of a Certain Age;* Otto Kernberg, *Internal World and External Reality;* Roger Gould, *Transformations* (New York: Simon and Schuster, 1978).

11. The death of a child who has served a reparative role in replacing an earlier relationship of significance for the mother is discussed by Charles Orbach, "The Multiple Meanings of the Loss of a Child," *American Journal of Psychotherapy, 13,* no. 4 (1959): 906-915.

12. Paul Chodoff, Stanford Friedman, and David Hamburg, "Stress, Defenses and Coping Behavior: Observations in Parents of Children with Malignant Disease," *American Journal of Psychiatry, 120,* no. 8 (1964): 743-749. One problem for children conceived shortly after the death of another child is the possibility of becoming a replacement or substitute. For example, see Albert Cain and Barbara Cain, "On Replacing a Child," *Journal of Child Psychiatry, 13,* no. 3 (1964): 443-456.

13. Herman Feifel, *New Meanings of Death* (New York: McGraw-Hill, 1977): p. 37.

14. Sigmund Freud, "On Transcience," *Standard Edition, 14* (London: Hogarth Press, 1957, originally published 1916).

four

Disorganization

This chapter, and the two that follow, focus on the process of mourning. We join the women at the beginning, when they have just received the news of the child's death, and go with them through the struggle and gradual adjustment.

These individual experiences help to explain the universal dynamics. The story belongs partly to all the women, but completely to none.

IMPACT

> I heard them talking. I just climbed out of bed and walked downstairs with no robe on or anything. Just my nightie and there they were. Two policemen and a priest. I just looked at them.
>
> (Marcia)

> I came part way downstairs and I could see the Navy, the feet, and . . . I figured that the plane had crashed because I knew the Navy didn't come unless someone was dead.
>
> (Jane)

The recollections of learning the news of the death are vivid. The women remember the first moments—the shoes of the Navy officers who came to the door; the light on the police car as it pulled up to the house at three in the morning; the look on her oldest son's face as he entered the house early Christmas day, having been the first to hear; or the words of the nurse on the telephone.

The parents were notified in person or called, at home and at work, on beautiful July mornings and on rainy April nights. Those that were told that the child was in the hospital but not that he or she was dead, rushed there, finding out when they arrived. The women who went to the hospitals were responding to an emergency, not necessarily a death. They frequently recalled, "I didn't even put my contacts in," or "I threw on the clothes that were next to the bed and didn't wear any underwear." The social amenities disappeared and the personal vanities were suspended without even being noticed. It was only later that they remembered these things with amusement and surprise—at the time it was not that they didn't care; they didn't even know.

Some went to the hospital or morgue already knowing the child was dead but wanting to see their son or daughter or needing to make an identification. Still others stayed at home. The deaths occurred in many ways, and the news was delivered differently, and yet the reactions of the women were surprisingly alike. Many said they sat down—on the floor, on the stairs, or in a chair. Anne fell down and remembered thinking that she must immediately pack all the family's belongings because they had to run away. The responses of sitting, falling, and running are reactions to severe shock, the physiological impact of hearing the news that is received as a physical blow. For some, there were immediate pain reactions. In some instances, the experience was literally physical, noted previously in bereavement studies.[1]

Julia was the only one who telephoned the hospital and checked to see if the news was true. This may have to do with being told by another of her children rather than the police or a medical authority. The women who received the news from police, husbands, or hospitals never questioned the truth of what they were being told, although some say they simultaneously did not believe it.

Most of the women do not remember crying until later. The phenomenon is shock, the physiological and psychological reactions to stimulus that threatens to overwhelm the individual. The response is to reject the event until it can be integrated in a slower, less frightening way. Survivors of natural disasters have been noted as numb, and it is understood as a way to prevent the excessive stimulation of the experience.[2] This kind of trauma leads to disorganization rather than regression.[3] Disorganization is a form of adaptation to trauma, the symptoms including listlessness, depression, startle reactions, recurrent nightmares, fears, and unsteadiness in relationships and in work. The symptoms result from "shrunken inner resources" and "ego contraction" as a response to events in the outer world, not neurotic or psychotic conflicts. In studies of soldiers in combat during World War II, complete disorganization occurred if they were not removed from the field. In shock, the ego processes erect a barrier to protect the women from greater harm. It is not a voluntary response nor is it under one's control. It is an initial rejection of change in response to an overwhelming situation.

A number of researchers note shrieking as part of the initial reaction. In this study there was only one instance of screaming and that was in the case of Lydia, who actually found her daughter's body after a fatal drug overdose. She said,

> I just went crazy. I couldn't tell you how long. It might have been two minutes, it might have been twenty. I just ran around the house screaming.

This difference may be a personality variable because Lydia is an excitable, expressive women, or it may be related to the additional shock of actual confrontation; it may be a combination of both.

Although the initial shock lasts only a short time, the accompanying numbness, prolonged periods of sitting, or in some cases agitation, and "zombielike" behavior persists. Simultaneously with the shock come varying degrees of disbelief; the news is incomprehensible. Most women said that for a long time they did not believe that their child was dead. Anne said, a year later, "I'm not sure that I believe it now." Sylvia was one of the few women who said she believed immediately that her daughter was dead, but awakened every night for weeks, got out of bed, found the newspaper account of the death, and read it over and over again. "To me, that was my way of saying it really did happen, it did. It made my mind realize it happened, it really happened."

The shock appeared to fade quickly for these women, but the disbelief persists in lessening degrees for a long time, even though actions taken and decisions made addressed the reality of the death.

THE EARLY DAYS: PASSIVITY AND PLANS

> They come up to you and they say, "Where do you want to bury your kid?" Where? I said, "Bury her with my father in Chicago" . . . . Then we ordered a thing, you know, whatever I ordered. Then I thought, no, I can't put her there because there is pollution. I thought, I don't want her breathing that bad air in the city, so we cancelled that. I mean you are just doing these weird things.
>
> (Anne)

The early days of mourning are a time of competing pressures of passivity and decisions. These days bridge the early period of disorganization and the later, lengthy struggle of holding on/letting go, having dynamics of both stages. The passivity continues, marked by obedience to authorities. Decision making is unknowingly impaired, concentration is difficult, and daily chores are often overwhelming and unmanageable. The women's energy and attention are totally absorbed by mourning. This was manifested in the early days by immersion in specific tasks and details pertaining to the death, such as notifying others and making funeral plans.

The women found that they behaved, for days and even weeks, with passivity and submission. They were particularly obedient to doctors, ministers, and funeral directors, the people who were especially influential during the first days. The medical doctors, in particular, stand out as having enormous authority. When the mother is completely helpless to do anything for her child, doctors assume even greater importance than usual. Any medical treatments that were suggested for those children who did not die instantly were agreed to even if they were not understood. In two instances, women exercised initiative with regard to medical treatment, telling doctors that no extraordinary means of life support were to be used after it became clear that the brain damage was extensive. The other request that was made by three women was donation of the body or organs. One woman was attempting to carry out a request of her son's that had been made a long time before. The others were nurses and familiar with hospital procedures. They felt that it was some consolation if the transplant could be carried out. It was possible in two instances, and Sylvia said that it helped to think that some good had come out of her daughter's accident.

The general passivity and inability to take initiative results from conditions of extreme stress. There is a strong regressive pull in situations that are both foreign and fearful, plus concentration of the ego processes due to the shock of this event. It is not surprising to see reliance on specialized authorities when the parents are helpless to change the situation.

It is also understandable that reactions to assistance would be mixed. Some were extremely grateful for the help from doctors, nurses, funeral directors, ministers, and other professionals who aided them in making plans or acted for them. Others remain angry at the treatment they received from these authorities. It is a complicated situation. The women are passive and looking to be told what to do; the professionals have erected their own individual and systemic defenses to enable them to deal with death; and the clash of these conflicting needs results in prolonged hostility on the part of some women. The ministers who "don't understand death," funeral directors who were cold, doctors and nurses who behaved in businesslike ways, all added to the mothers' misery and anger. It is impossible to distinguish how much of the anger is justifiably a result of professional mistakes or lack of caring, and how much is the families' response to their own helplessness.

The parents' passivity and helplessness clashing with helping institutions is poignantly illustrated in the conflict over seeing the child's body. Louise recalls:

> My husband was the only one that really verbalized the fact that he wanted to see Larry. I think that we all probably did, but we went in there hearing that we weren't going to. So we just accepted that very easily. Don didn't question it very much. He just said, "Well, I want to see him." They'd say, "Well, it's better that you don't. We don't want you to." So he just, he stood there in the door just like a whipped puppy . . . I never considered the fact of going against what they told us.

Louise remains sorry that she did not see her son. Even a delay in seeing the child's body can engender bitter feelings. Sandy was told to wait because he needed to "be cleaned up" and that disrespect still rankles 2½ years later. All the women who did see their children felt satisfied at their decision to do so. Even if the child looked different, it appeared to have helped settle the reality of the death in the mother's mind and reduce the tormenting fantasies of what the child might have looked like. When the child looked different, the women said it was all right because the image that she retains is that of a living child, not a dead one. Jane was articulate on this point and is convinced that it helped her to accept the death, a feeling shared by others. Based on his work with mothers of stillborns and neonatal deaths, Davidson advocates letting the decision rest with the mother. If she chooses to see the child, he suggests presenting the baby wrapped as a live infant. He found that it reduced the incidence of fantasied crying that some mothers experienced.[4] Patty, who saw her daughter, and Anne, who did not, were the only two who heard voices. Anne decided not to see her daughter, a model, because

> All I could think of was that she was so beautiful, and she was so vain that she would not want anyone to see her dead. I did not want to see her dead . . . and I'm glad that I did it for her sake because she was very vain . . . .

Seeing the child helped to reduce anxiety and fantasies. The women who saw their children voiced strong beliefs that it was important to them. They were satisfied with that decision. Those who did not have lingering questions about whether that decision made their bereavement more difficult. Whether or not to see the child becomes one of the first in a series of decisions which exemplify the helplessness and submissiveness to others that extended to life in general during this time.

The women generally report sitting around passively, stunned. A few of them called themselves "zombies." They wandered through the first days, doing what they were told. Sandy remembered being told to take a nap, so she and her husband walked obediently into the bedroom and laid down. It took several minutes before she realized that she wasn't tired and questioned what she was doing.

There is little available strength to argue with others. Sylvia had so many people at the hospital with her that after several hours she and her husband announced they were leaving. They got into the car, drove home, walked into the house and out again, and went back to the hospital. When they got there, enough time had elapsed that her friends had left. The purpose of the trip home had been because she wanted to be alone and wasn't able to say so.

Chores like cooking and cleaning were unmanageable for days and weeks. Grocery shopping was often postponed until there was no food in the house, and then it was a difficult event.

These actions illustrate the intense passivity of this early time. There also was usually a numbness that had the effect of protecting the women from much that was going on around her. This numbness and zombielike feeling can also be a deep identification with death. Some women have anxiety reactions instead of the immobility described. Increased activity, caring for others, or an inability to be still is not uncommon, and is an anxiety response to the death.

At a time when decisions are difficult to make, certain ones, such as telling the children, family, and friends, and funeral plans, become critical. The women's descriptions of these decisions show how they immersed themselves in the details of funeral plans and informing other children. Marion remembers,

> We wanted "Fire and Rain" to be played at the memorial service, and the minister, well, he wasn't all that thrilled about it. He said the organist said "I don't think we have the sheet music," and we said, "We'll get it." So we were trying, we were calling. Finally a friend of ours said . . . she'd pick it up. I remember that was a big deal. We had to get that.

The decisions, too, about telling other people assume great importance. Marcia talked about her preoccupation that first night in deciding how to tell her remaining son, the family, and the community. At three in the morning, she and her husband sat:

> We didn't call anybody. We tried to figure out how . . . were we going to tell this 16-year-old kid? We knew that whatever we did, it was important. It was not only important for our family . . . for all the families that would be involved . . . I didn't believe it was real . . . . It's like being chairman of a committee, you've got to get something on paper.

"Chairman of a committee" sounds remarkably detached and unfeeling, yet that is precisely the recurring experience of some women during the early days. They report going through the motions, sometimes with the feeling of sitting on their own shoulders and watching themselves. The detachment appears to be a vestige of shock, but far diminished from the initial impact.

In looking back on the decisions of the first night or day, some were wise, others irrational, but at the time they appeared to make sense. The choices made were important to them then and afterward, particularly since many had repercussions that could not be appreciated at the time. In these early days, they seemed aware that decisions would matter later but they had no way of knowing the future consequences.

In addition to the need to make certain decisions, the absorption served another purpose for the family: It enabled them to move from a passive to an active position. They still had control over something and clung to it fiercely. Decision making focused time and emotions that otherwise would have been occupied by the loss. Helplessness threatens to overwhelm the mourner and many actions and thoughts throughout the mourning process are attempts to alleviate the helpless state.

The early days also saw the emergence of physical symptoms which varied for each woman in form, intensity, and duration. Most of them described initial physical pain that faded into an enduring sensation of emptiness lasting at least as long as a year, often in the chest or stomach area. Intense grief often leads to feelings of emptiness, but for mothers this intense and lingering sensation might be related to mothering itself and a time when, in fact, the child shared the mother's body. The nonexistence of the child is reflected by the emptiness inside the mother and is symptomatic of her longing for the child. This emptiness, when considered in light of the biological connection of mother and child and the sustained symbiotic relationship is reminiscent of amputees who report "phantom limbs" after surgery.

There is also an exacerbation of previous conditions in these women. Those women who had trouble sleeping before the death had increased trouble afterward. Several women who never had trouble sleeping found that they "fell asleep everywhere" during the early phase of mourning. The fatigue and exhaustion recounted by all is related to depression and lasted intermittently for at least a year. Marion remembered "crawling back into bed" after her husband left in the morning, and saving her strength for going out to see friends and for the evenings when her husband returned.

Some reported eating more and gaining weight, some lost weight, again related to predisposition. For most, eating assumed the same mechanical quality as other activities during the early days. It did not occur to most of them to eat, but if someone gave them food, they generally complied and ate. They were grateful to friends and family who brought food into the house and felt reassured that the children were eating.

Other physical symptoms that were heightened by the death were headaches and high blood pressure in women prone to these problems. Two women said they drank more than usual. Most of these problems diminished after the first year to levels approximate to those before the death. The major persistent symptom was the lack of energy and vitality, most likely related to depression.

Several women noted that they were afraid to take medication during this time. They feared becoming addicted to anything that would provide relief from the emotional and physical experience, and did not trust themselves to be moderate, so they abstained from all drugs.

In closing this chapter on the early days of mourning, we look at the funeral plans. Services mean many things. The planning of the funeral illustrates another significant dimension of early mourning, disbelief.

The women thought very much about others (friends, family, and community) when making funeral plans. The importance of the "right" funeral was a concern, partly because it was something they could do for themselves and the child when there was little else to do. But it was also a statement—in some cases a tribute—to the child's life or personality. Readings and songs were carefully chosen as a reflection of the child. Anne insisted on a private funeral because she could not bear to have anyone around her or seeing her daughter dead. Marcia had a service and invited 500 people back to her house as a way of staying in touch with her daughter's love of life and exuberance. It would be a mistake to discount these events as exclusively being defenses against death and fear. The women noted that the services were for the child, in memory of the life as well as marking the death. In some ways, the child was still alive to the mother and other family members and the funeral was arranged to meet with the child's approval. They knew this in some instances and said they actively sought to carry out what they believed to be the dead child's wishes.

The funeral here reflects one way of assuming mastery in a helpless situation, as a reflection of the child's life and personality, as an example of the decision making that must go on. Within the description, the pervasive qualities of disbelief are also seen. Disbelief fades in power and intensity, but attests to the lingering inability to accept the total lack of further existence for someone who is loved. It is necessary to remain aware of the intense difficulty in accepting the finality of death, particularly when the person has been a part of one's life and self. For these women, disbelief took many forms and lasted a year or longer. In the early days we see Sylvia reading the news clipping to remind herself that it really happened, but continuing to wait for the school bus each day. Louise waited for letters to come from college. Most women "saw" the child in mistakes of identity.

Some of the women reacted with annoyance when they found themselves "playing games" or "pretending" as they called it. Others said they knew they were pretending and occasionally allowed themselves to indulge in fantasies, although it embarrassed them. They knew their children had died, but were intolerant when confronted with the persistence of unconscious wishes seen in dreams, mistaken identities, slips of the tongue, and clinging to the daily connections that have been broken by change.

> You don't really realize they're lost forever right at the beginning. You keep thinking . . . she's coming back sometimes . . . . It's not for a long time that you really come to grips with that.
>
> (Deborah)

The responses seen in the early days change quickly in important ways. Immediate reactions of shock, numbness, passivity, and disbelief are primarily related to the impact of loss. But there is a rapid shift in focus to the meaning of that particular loss, the special child to that mother. That changing emphasis is apparent, and the long struggle remaining in the mourning process is a personal adjustment to a very special loss.

NOTES

1. George Pollock, "Mourning and Adaptation"; Colin Murray Parkes, *Bereavement: Studies in Adult Life.*

2. Robert J. Lifton, *The Broken Connection.*

3. Abraham Kardiner, "Traumatic Neuroses of War," *American Handbook of Psychiatry, 1* (1959): 249-257.

4. Glen Davidson, "Understanding: Death of the Wished-for Child" (Springfield, IL: *OGR Service Corporation,* 1979).

five

Holding On/Letting Go

Loss is not accepted without a struggle. In bereavement, it becomes necessary to grapple with the difficult internal work of adjusting to a world in which the loved child no longer exists. The testing of reality repeatedly demonstrates the finality of death and requires that prior attachment be withdrawn.

This chapter examines the conflicts of the lengthy, painful process of holding on/letting go. It is a period of testing the past against the present. The women learn which aspects of the child can be kept, and which must be relinquished in favor of their own development.

It is common to think of children as receiving a legacy from parents, but here is the legacy, often painful, that is left by the child. These women are left to complete their mothering alone, in the best ways that they can. They assume the double task of keeping memories alive while they let go of the child as a living member of the family. They do it for the child, but they do it too, for themselves: to complete unfinished business. A clear illustration of the process is found in the phenomena of memorials, those acts intended to preserve the child's memory.

MEMORIALS

I had this little thing printed up here because I liked it so well . . . I gave it to a lot of people. I don't know, I felt like I was spreading his

> little prayer around. People could keep it and remember him by it. I don't want him forgotten.
>
> (Louise)

The funeral service is one of the first places where the struggle of holding on/letting go can be seen. Ellen spoke for many when she said,

> When they stood outside in the rain waiting just to get inside the funeral home, we were very, very proud of her. It was a tribute to her.

A well-attended funeral service becomes the earliest reassurance that others remember and care enough to come out in the rain, on crutches, to wait in line, or to take time off work. It is one of the rare instances when the quantity of assurance was its own reward.

For some, it is particularly gratifying to have the child's friends and siblings' friends attend the service or visit the house. Adults are often assumed to attend the service out of affection for the parents or from social responsibility, but children's presence is taken as proof that the peers cared and lives had been touched by the child. It is important that the young person live on in the memories of people outside the family. Memories are one of the few aspects of immortality for anyone, so for an individual who has not lived a long life, and has neither children nor work to leave behind, the memories held by others assume added significance.

The young people become, to the mother, a symbol of hope and continuity. Any feelings of envy, resentment, or jealousy that other children are alive generally surface later, but as a part of memorializing the dead child, services, attendance of young people, and testimonials reflective of the child, are reassuring to the mother. In the first public act of letting go, some compensation is received in knowing others will remember.

Another manifestation of the difficulty in letting go of the child is seen in the preservation of the room, sometimes for a while, sometimes for years, often rationalizing that the space was not needed. Some mothers packed up everything immediately, "the next morning while I was still numb. If I had waited, I never would have done it." It is not unusual to find rooms unused 2 years later, particularly where there are no pressures of living space to force the issue.

Even when the rooms were changed, there is the dilemma of what to keep and what to give away. Often siblings took the clothes or rearranged the room. Sometimes mothers gave the clothes to "children who needed them. It was fine as long as I never saw them." Who received the child's things was important. Pieces of jewelry, mementos, and personal items were given to the child's close friends, clearly as remembrances. Occasionally it was a child who entered the mother's life later, and who in some way was identified with the dead child, who became the beneficiary.

During the meeting with Sylvia, she worked on a lovely pink-and-white patchwork quilt that had been intended for the 18-year-old daughter who had died. The girl had been the youngest of six and the only daughter. The two had been very close and shared personality characteristics and career goals. Sylvia said that the quilt had been started for her daughter, at the girl's insistence, prior to her death, exactly 4 years before. She had just recently picked it up again,

> I'll never use it probably, but I'll get it done. I intended to do it one time so I'll do it sometime, but I couldn't do it right away.

The quilt had multiple mearnings. Her daughter had gotten her started on quilting; it was an interest they shared; it was to be for her daughter; and it was a reproduction of one that Sylvia herself had used and loved as a child. Finishing that quilt was a way to keep one aspect of the relationship alive. It did not matter very much what use the quilt would ultimately have but, "maybe if I have a granddaughter . . . ."

These few examples of memorials portray how the mothers perpetuate the child's life through memories and actions, while simultaneously coming to grips with the finality of death. There are many examples of this dynamic, each unique because it is integrally related to that child and mother. The pattern is one in which the mother assumes the responsibility for the continuity of the child's spirit through acts of her own making.

Over time memorials take on different forms. Sherry and the other mothers who lost daughters in the same accident used community donations to upgrade certain sports facilities the girls had liked. Marcia and her husband set up a scholarship for an all-around high-school girl: "It's the spirit of what she represents . . . it should go on." Jane gives a scholarship to the Boy Scouts, and Lydia, whose daughter died of a drug overdose, became involved in working with behaviorally disordered adolescents. Specific memorials are based, in part, on the mother's identification with the child. The aspect of identification explains why memorials do not fade quickly, but change over time, in form and intensity. The complex ways that the child is internalized, and the death influential in the mothers' lives, are deeply felt for years.

Accepting the death is a lengthy process, aided by those memorials that keep the child alive to the mother and others. The acts seen here bridge the distance between mother and child as the essential withdrawal takes place. But separation does not occur all at once. It happens again and again with each reminder of the death.

REACTIONS TO EVOCATIVE STIMULI

> Sunday was our (surviving) daughter's graduation from high school . . . and it rained, so it was inside and it was hot. And there sitting all these young kids, and the address had to do with looking toward the future, and Sam and I were sitting there crying.
>
> (Jane)

During the initial shock only certain powerful stimuli are received, but this protection of numbness is quickly replaced by an acute sensitivity. The women experience themselves as raw and subject to easy distress by a variety of known and undefinable precipitators. All are associated with the child and set off intense reactions.

Many events are common to the mothers; others are idiosyncratic, bound up in the meaning of the child, the relationship, and the circumstances of the death. For most, the child's birthday and the anniversary of the death are painful days. The birthday, which had been joyous, can become more difficult than the anniversary of the death, an event with already existing painful associations.

The same is often true of weddings and funerals. Weddings, because they are happy, are more of a reminder of the loss and deprivation. These events assume greater significance if they are related specifically to the child's death, for example, the wedding of a friend or peer of the child, or a funeral for another child, even a stranger. The chance of experiencing more painful affects is closely tied to the intimacy of the remainder.

Holidays were another common problem, especially during the first year. The mothers handled the occasions differently, but commented, "That first Christmas was a bitch!", "we ran!", and "We put a Christmas tree on his grave." Preparations were additionally difficult because the women still fought physical and emotional fatigue and depression.

Other precipitators of intense emotions also appear regularly, often connected to remembering the death or fearing another. For Louise, it was her daughter's graduation from college. The son who had died was to have been the first of the children to receive a degree; the daughter was now passing him by. That event had generated anxiety, awakening the fear that "I haven't gotten through the teens," as if one not having made it may mean no one will. Passing the scene of the accident or hearing about another similar one can reactivate the sadness. Having a child come home late can set off recollections of the night and fears that it will happen again. The passing of the school bus at a certain time of day, or the hour when the child arrived home from school, are only two more examples of the brutal reminders occurring on a frequent basis. These women have learned that they are not invulnerable to tragedy. The safety of thinking that these things happen to "other people" is not a reliable defense for them.

Yet other precipitators are more specific. Certain birthdays, for example, 16, 18, or 21, ages that the child was looking forward to as a marker for driving, voting, or independence, take on even more meaning. This is aggravated by comparisons with the remaining children, who may not appreciate that birthday or occasion as much as the dead child would have or is imagined to have responded. Marion noted that she had trouble adjusting to her youngest son, Ed, passing his dead brother's age:

> Ed is now 20. Ed was always the youngest and now Sean is always locked into age 19. With Ed moving into that, the scheme was off. It wasn't right, you know, it wasn't meant to be.

Where it all stopped becomes significant because it makes the mother again aware of what never will be. Any changes in the family, such as these illustrations, remind her that she cannot hold on to the past as it was.

The most difficult reminders are those that are unexpected. Because the child was so integral to her life, the ordinary triggers are numerous—signing names to Christmas cards, setting the table, being asked, "How many children do you have?", passing special foods in the supermarket, college catalogues arriving in the mail, photographs, or scraps of paper and notes left to be discovered later. The shock of the unexpected reminder brings it all back. Deborah recalled,

> I went to New York with my husband on business right after she was killed, just for diversion (and) was going up the escalator at Lord &

> Taylor there, and you know, came off and here were all clothes for her age, and I just turned and bolted down the up escalator. I just couldn't face it.

The women learn quickly which stimuli will cause distressing emotional reactions. Then they can avoid or seek them out, depending on their needs and circumstances. Several tried to avoid the scene of the accident, holiday rituals, and other reminders at those times when they felt unable to face the resulting emotions. At other times, particularly when they were alone, they listened to specific music or handled the child's possessions, visited the room, looked at photographs, and let the emotions flow. What plagued them, right from the beginning and continuing for years, was the unexpected event that caught them completely off guard and unprepared. In spite of the precautions taken, their days contained many incidents for which there was no protection.

The characteristic shared by the variety of stimuli examined here is that each triggers associations to the child that died or to the mother/child relationship. Many of the associations remain out of awareness, but the result is an intense emotional response.

Some of these types of responses have been termed anniversary reactions, manifestations of incompleted or deviant mourning. An anniversary reaction is a day, time, date, or significant event that acts as a trigger to repressed memories. As a result, symptoms, either behaviors or emotions, are seen.[1]

In examining evocative stimuli, the concentration has been on those precipitators that intrude into the mother's life. There is, within this general phenomenon, another dynamic where the mother actually assumes an active role in an attempt to search for the lost child, for example, the woman who seeks a blond, blue-eyed foster child to replace her own. These attempts, conscious or unconscious, indicate a yearning and striving to recover the son or daughter. The active search predominates early in the mourning process, but passive aspects continue indefinitely. It has been suggested that it is not only the object that is experienced as lost, but the survivor, in this instance the mother, who also feels lost.

Both the reactions to unsolicited stimuli and the searching predominate strongly early in the mourning process because they are tied into hope. Slowly comes the realization that nothing can be done to undo the loss. For many mothers, this dawning knowledge is intolerable.

GOING CRAZY AND THE WISH TO DIE

> I would say, I wish we could just all die. I just didn't wanna be alive, and I figured if we all went at once, then there wouldn't be any of us left to have to go through this again. I was the only one that wanted to do it. The kids didn't think that it was a very good idea.
>
> (Betty)

It is not unusual to hear a bereaved mother discuss her fears of "going crazy," "not being able to handle it," "breaking down" and "never coming back." The fear of going crazy is usually related to the intensity of the emotional reactions after the child's death and is perceived, by some women, as a serious threat at certain periods during that first year. The women believed that they would not be able to tolerate the stress and intense emotions of the bereavement experience.

The fear of "going crazy" is an anxiety response. It fulfills a certain psychodynamic function in the individual. Popular thinking accords insane people four general characteristics: no restraint of emotions and actions, especially anger and rage; memory defects and lack of comprehension; relief from the usual adult responsibilities; and removal from the home to an institution.[2]

Anxiety is usually the basis for fears of losing one's sanity. It is easy to see the appeal of "going crazy" as an escape from an intolerable situation. The desire to escape is also seen in the expressed wish to "trade places" with the child. Trading places gives the mother some mastery over the situation, allows the child to live out a full life, but also relieves the mother of having to go on without her son or daughter. Lydia noted,

> . . . when I die, I'm not going to have to deal with anybody. It's the people left that have to deal with the loss. I'm much more frightened of the loss than I am of my own death.

The wish to die and thoughts of death have previously been considered an identification with the dead,[3] but suggested here is the accompanying wish to renounce the burden of living and, like "going crazy," a relief from emotions and responsibility. For these women, surviving had a painfully high price. The fear of "going crazy," an anxiety reaction, and the wish to die, a symptom of depression, reflect both those conditions existing in normal bereavement.

Death also means reunion with the child. Interestingly, Mandy, who had often wished to die that first year, faced a series of tests for cancer, and then realized the strength of her wish to live. The resolution of this guilt inducing ambivalence comes, for some, through faith in eventual reunion.

FAITH

> She's got to be in Heaven. I imagine that she had to be calmed down a bit up there. She really was a very strong personality.
>
> (Marcia)

> I have this worry that I didn't know where he stood in his relationship with God.
>
> (Betty)

> She is in a box under the ground. We live and we die. The only difference between me and my cat is that I am aware of life and my cat is merely living life. No, I will never see her again. She is gone. She does not exist.
>
> (Anne)

Mothers, confronted with the death of their own children, rarely espouse a general religious dogma. They have been forced to examine personal beliefs and tend to rely on a faith that is based only in part on organized religious training. Those who believed in a form of Heaven and God before the death still believed, maybe more strongly than before. Those who did not had no change of mind. Because beliefs about an afterlife tend to be idiosyncratic, the women voiced different fantasies and concerns.

Very few women were adamant that there is no Heaven, no afterlife, and that existence totally ceases with death. But for these few mothers, their belief meant that there is no hope of reunion with their children. Most women believe in "something," were questioning their ideas, or were certain that the child was in Heaven or a "pleasant place." Julia and Betty worried whether their sons had made it to Heaven but felt fairly confident that they were not in Hell. Others were sure, and

Louise said that she was living her life very carefully to insure getting to Heaven herself. She did not want to take the chance of not seeing her son again. Betty and Frances wondered how they would recognize their children when they were reunited. Several women portrayed Heaven as a place where the child was "doing her own thing" much like he or she had done while alive, still watching the family when they were engaged in activities in which the child had been an important participant. Several others imagined the child with someone else, and the company was often another person who had also died prematurely—a companion of the child's, a friend of the mother's, or the child of a friend. It is an intriguing phenomenon that people who die before their time are assumed to be with others who were similarly caught. One speculation is that it is related to the tendency of people to seek out similarly afflicted others in times of crisis. The mothers had also done this, finding comfort in the companionship of other bereaved mothers. It was reassuring for them to think of the child, separated from the family, with someone friendly and understanding. In this fantasy, the security they could not provide was eternally assured. The belief in Heaven provides that union and fantasy of wholeness which could overcome the loss.

In spite of faith or, in some cases, because of it, the women expressed their anger at God. Marion said that when she was told that her son was "in God's hands," her response was "God has no right having him." And Lydia followed a similar thought with, "So what am I supposed to do with this hole in my soul?" Others said they would not dream of questioning God and, related to unfailing belief, some said that without faith they would not have been able to make it, "(You) have to believe to keep your sanity." Losing faith means being left with no answers and no reasons. In the face of their own helplessness, there is the strong need to believe in a continuing existence for the child and God's will. Personal impotence is mitigated by the faith that there was a plan even if it was unknowable to the mother.

Most of the women had more than faith in an afterlife to keep them in touch with their children. Holding "conversations" with the child was a way of maintaining a connection for years.

CONNECTIONS IN HEAVEN

> Sometimes, walking the dog at night I'll just chat with Sean. I might say something like, it depends on my mood, 'God, Sean, isn't this a

bitch?' The conversations aren't always around the same thing. I mean I'm not saying, 'Pick up your clothes.'

(Marion)

The conversations are casual, telling the child about something that happened during the day, sharing the sadness or loneliness, and, in angry or depressed moods, rebuking the child for dying.

Several women described asking the child for a favor, similar to what they would have requested if the child had lived. For example, "Watch out for your sister," or "You're in a position to look after your brother." Louise explained it as, "I'm his mother. I have the right to ask."

These women now have a personal connection in Heaven, an interesting dynamic acknowledging and denying the death. The child is in Heaven, therefore dead, but expected to continue as a family member, being in an even better position to carry out his or her responsibilities. The women who described this connection are, not surprisingly, those who believe in an afterlife.

Other women, regardless of religious belief or faith, reported hearing voices or actually seeing the child. This has been documented in previous bereavement studies but without the persistence seen here. Visions, voices and conversations have been noted as particularly strong when the death was unexpected, giving the survivor little chance to prepare for separation.[4] The incidences of hearing voices, seeing images, and carrying on conversations appear to be phenomena of intense but normal grief reactions in child loss.

In examining the adjustment to a child's death and hypothesizing about some of the meanings that underlie these observations, the magnitude of this loss continues to emerge. The impact of the child's death, with the resulting helplessness, forces the women to resort to a variety of coping strategies in the attempt to reestablish an equilibrium. We continue with other dynamics that function to restore the mothers' sense of mastery.

SUPERSTITION

That was the first weekend ever I did not worry; did not even have a premonition. We were sitting and playing cards when the accident

> happened, or we were talking, one of the two, with my sister and brother-in-law. Just nothing, no premonition things were wrong.
>
> (Mandy)

It is always somewhat of a surprise to glimpse the superstitions that comfortably coexist with reason. Several of the women provide some interesting examples of the fears and wishes connected to death and mothering.

The fact that the mothers had no idea of the tragedy that was occurring is not unusual. Their belief that they *should have known* is surprising. They felt that there should have been a premonition of the event. It raises the speculation that women who generally consider themselves sensitive, good mothers truly expect, in some magical way, to "know" what is going on with their children. This belief begins to make sense if we go back to the earliest communication between mother and child, the wordless symbiotic attachment of pregnancy and early development. This aspect of early mothering, coupled with the omnipotence of the "ideal mother," seems to linger on in the form of surprise and guilt that she did not know when the child was in trouble and needing her. Guilt is present because of the belief that she should have known, not have been so separate as to be able to sleep or enjoy herself without any thought of the child.

As an aspect of maternal bereavement, superstitions can be understood as the continuing attempt to master tragic circumstance by making sense out of the uncontrollable and unreasonable event. The helplessness, so difficult to accept, is compensated for by the wish to have suspected death. If they had known, they fantasize, the accident could have been prevented, or, at least, they could have provided comfort for the child. Not to have warning or knowledge is another affront to the protective function of being a mother. To harbor the belief that she can know when loved ones are in need is to insure the mother's sense of safety and provide reassurance that she will never be caught off guard and helpless. It is easy to forget, in a society as advanced and sophisticated as ours, that primitive beliefs and wishes are still with us and are used in controlling the demons.

In relinquishing the physical presence of the child, the retention of personal objects and possessions, creation of living memorials, and secure heavens have been shown. One striking pattern that emerged in the mothers' attempts to keep the child is that of holding specific visual images.

FROZEN FRAMES

> It's like when she looked down and said, "Goodbye," and I said, "Be careful now, it's icy. Watch it." "Oh, I will, Mom," is forever frozen in my mind. The smile.
>
> (Anne)

The lasting visual images came to be described as "frozen frames" because of the visual clarity of the recollection and the fact that the images are selected and retained from the many available to be recalled. Memories of the child, stories, and vignettes are part of any bereavement, but in addition to the general collection of anecdotes, two distinct but interrelated patterns consistently emerged.

The first "frame" is the moment described in Chapter Four, hearing the news. The faces, clothes, words, smells, or weather remain vivid, very often retrievable at will. The second "frame" is an image of the last, or close to last, time that the mother spent with a living child. These were isolated occurrences, each different, with the commonality being that the incident, however trivial to others, has this special meaning for the mother. These women would not, under ordinary circumstances, have remembered the smile, the exchange of casual greetings, or the seating arrangements if the child had lived. Those details would have been filed away with the innumerable trivia one notes casually each day.

It is not possible to assess whether the images are actual reproductions of past interactions or screen memories. Either way, the women have particular images that remain alive. Previous research has noted the preoccupation with thoughts of the dead and visual images, but tends to classify sustaining images with pathological reactions. This study presents contrary evidence and questions whether previous research has been too hasty in categorizing pathology and may have underestimated the duration of the mourning process in cases of unexpected child loss.

The distinct patterns of the "frozen frames" have also raised questions about existing explanations. Neiderland, in his work with concentration camp survivors, defined hypermnesia as the survivor's overly sharp, distinct, and indelible memories as far as persecution events are concerned. He explains it as the opportunity to relive the event, assuming a more active role and thereby changing the outcome.[5] Certainly, reviewing the event contains the wish to master it. More manipulation is possible over fantasy than over reality, and in a helpless situation this dynamic is expected to come into prominence. In widows, it was noted that they conduct an "obsessional review," dwelling on events leading up to the death.[6] This also provides a rehearsal for future events. Perhaps with preparation the outcome could be different if confronted again.

A somewhat different explanation is put forth by Wolfenstein in describing victims of disasters. She states that "tormenting memories" allow the mourner to gradually accustom one's self to an initially overwhelming experience.[7]

While the phenomenon of "frozen frames" is consistent with both explanations, the dual theme of separation and sharing time together suggests a broader dynamic being enacted. The images appear to be frozen because a profound period of time was ended and begun.

Very recently, preliminary research with animals has suggested that emotional events release hormones that act on the brain as a "fixative," ensuring that whatever is happening at the time will be remembered for a while.[8]

The women in this study did not see their children die, and were unprepared. Most saw the child after death but have only fantasies of the death itself. They retain terrible images of what the child went through in the last moments. In unexpected deaths, there are always questions that cannot be answered. No matter how hard they tried to gather information about the incident, pieces of that time will remain unavailable.

The pattern of the first frame, hearing the news of the death, is the closest thing the mothers have to being there and witnessing the event. It was the moment of separation. The second pattern is the last living memory, the final link to the life before the tragedy and the last connection to a living child. All the women said that life had changed—the death created a before and after in their lives. Ordinary interactions become cherished moments because an important time ended there. When the change occurred, the images were frozen. These patterns capture the duality of the struggle: what can be kept and what must be relinquished. "Why?" Anne said, "It ended there. That was all I had left."

The myriad ways of holding on/letting go result from the intensity of the loss. The strength of identification with motherhood also increases the feelings of guilt, anger, and depression.

GUILT

> When I go to the cemetery, my thought was, 'Gee, I wish I could have, would have done more for him.' You know, I think that's why I'm even uncomfortable there—because I realize we made it pretty tough for you.
>
> (Thelma)

There are several different causes of guilt in maternal bereavement: (1) actual responsibility for the event; (2) imagined responsibility for not having prevented the death; (3) assuming blame for the child's responsibility of hurting himself, herself, or others; (4) as a reaction to being a survivor; or (5) relief in ending a conflicted relationship. These categories are not mutually exclusive.

Two women said they felt actual responsibility for negligence. Patty had been a nurse and believed she should have recognized her daughter's deteriorating condition, and Lydia was in graduate nurse's training to be a social worker and said there had been signs of her daughter's drug abuse but she had not wanted to see them. Guilt, in these instances, was further increased by professional failure.

Other than the two instances noted, the remainder of the deaths were accidents or homicides. The mothers of these victims emphasized their lack of guilt. Yet, all of the women still blamed themselves for not having bought the child a better car, not picking her up (thereby preventing the fatal ride with a friend), not keeping him at home instead of permitting a trip, and other variations of "What if . . . ." They repetitively recount all the things they could have done to prevent the child from being in that place at that time.

No mother said that she felt guilty over the child's responsibility, although in five cases the child was at the controls and others were hurt or killed. In these cases, blame was attributed to car malfunction, other drivers, or unavoidable accidents.

The guilt experienced as a result of surviving is a difficult area to explore. The triumph of being left alive remains the "inadmissible thought," but is manifested by the reluctance to separate the dead from the living and the symbolic search for repair, numerous examples of each having been presented.[9] Survival is unconsciously felt as a betrayal and just being alive can become a source of guilt. Earlier studies have linked guilt with the age of the survivor, but in this instance it is more the relationship that engenders the feeling.[10] A mother surviving a child is "wrong" to these women, just as it is "wrong" for a child to die.

The final cause of guilt seen in this group resulted from relief at ending a conflictual relationship. Thelma called it "double guilt," the guilt from having the child die coupled with feelings of relief. The women who spoke about this feeling were not the only ones who had conflictual relationships with their children. It appears that as an aspect of maternal bereavement, guilt is one of the emotions women find most difficult to discuss, and perhaps even to experience.

ANGER AND DEPRESSION

> Sometimes I start thinking about the people that actually killed him. I get a little bit upset over it but I have never really been angry.
>
> (Louise)

> A couple of times after I lost Dee, I went out in the car and just screamed at the top of my lungs.
>
> (Deborah)

All major studies and theoretical discussions of bereavement have included anger as a normal emotion during mourning,[11] most agreeing that it predominates as one separates from the loved person. The anger is a result of being left, implying the acknowledgment of the loss and the beginnings of acceptance. Interestingly, the women reported little or no anger. Many even commented that they had read about anger in books on bereavement but had not experienced it. Looking beyond the statements, we do see that the women who said they did not feel angry did have periods of scolding the dead child for being so stupid as to get himself or herself killed. They asked the child, "Why did you do this to me?" They said that their husbands were terribly angry. In two instances, the wife talked the husband out of pursuing legal actions. It appears that in some of the marital relationships, the husband becomes the one who expresses the anger more directly and wants to initiate action. The wife expresses her anger more subtly or pacifies her husband's anger.

Some of the deaths were directly attributable to another person, and even then the women said they were not angry. Deborah said that the only thing worse than losing a child would be to kill someone else's and therefore did not feel angry or revengeful. In other deaths, the exact circumstances remain unknown, but women tend toward the most generous explanations, such as, "It could have been my child driving."

Sometimes the anger is rationalized with "Other people are worse off," "He could have been a vegetable," "At least no one else was killed," and other variations on "It could have been worse."

Chapter Four noted the different individuals that were often the targets of anger in the early days—hospital personnel, ministers, funeral directors, unfeeling friends, or family. These people took the brunt of anger that comes from a helpless state. The anger at the early stage was based, in part, on the desire to perceive control as located in someone. So, initially, anger was directed at those who failed the mother or child. It changes slowly. The two women who were plaintiffs in law suits said that they were angry at the "attitude" afterward on the part of the driver or the school; it conveyed a lack of respect and value for the child. Sylvia expressed regret that she "had" to sue the other driver, and had he expressed remorse, she never would have filed suit.

The anger gradually becomes more diffuse, particularly for the women who have no one to blame. They cannot feel much satisfaction from being enraged with a falling tree, a malfunctioning car, the weather, bizarre circumstance, faceless people, or their own children. The anger that is so difficult to express is the rage at the unfairness of losing a child. The diffuseness, the protest, and the intense helplessness of the situation engendered a greater struggle with depression than with anger.

Depression is a fundamental response to death and loss. The women found themselves unresponsive and without vitality. The withdrawal in depression helped to conserve the energy that was needed for intense absorption of the mourning. Depression is characterized by a loss of interest in life's pleasures. The world may become more than uninteresting—it may seem unreal. A depressed mother knows that a loss occurred in the outer world, but more importantly, she experiences herself as impoverished. The loss is in the internal world as well as the external one.

Her behaviors are often constricted. But with this general conservation, the mother is preoccupied with one aspect of her life, in this case, the child's death. Her inner world is very busy, but the interest may be limited to the loss. Underlying the depression is a protest against the loss of the child and it can be a defense against the helplessness.

Lifton's conceptualization of depression contributes to our understanding of the reactions in bereavement. He focuses on the protest in depression. The protest is directed at the loss:

> What the protest seems to be saying is: we are defeated, inwardly dead, but we do not accept this state of things.

He goes on to note that it is not so much the ambivalence toward the dead, as Freud thought,

> as this terrible duality of simultaneous immersion in the deep sadness of irreplaceable loss and the perpetual, ineffectual protest against that loss.[12]

Helplessness is central in depression, with differences occurring in the manner in which individuals deal with it. It has its roots in earlier separations and signifies, in some sense, a separation from one's earliest loves. Depressive reactions include an inhibition of fight in the attempt to ward off further losses.[13]

Most of these women struggled with depression for a long time. They were fearful of new places and new people. Anyone or anything that threatened the connections to the child was dangerous, and living took them further away from the time their son or daughter was a living member of the family. The defense against helplessness has been central to the themes examined, and we have seen the variety of ways that the women attempted to assume mastery and reestablish meaning in their lives.

As the struggle proceeds, they begin to rebuild their lives without that child.

> When I look back at what I was, and what I am, I can see a big difference. That gives me some hope in the future. In a year from now, I'll be better than what I am now. I feel that someday, I'll probably be pretty close to what I was. Maybe never right there, but maybe pretty close.
>
> (Louise, almost 2 years later)

NOTES

1. There is a coupling of symptoms with a day, time, or event, but it is the internal determinants which are significant. The external referent serves only as a trigger. Described by George Pollock, "Temporal Anniversary Manifestations, Hour, Day, Holiday," *Psychoanalytic Quarterly, 40,* No.1 (1971): 123-131.

2. Henry Grand, "Fear of Becoming Insane," *American Journal of Psychotherapy, 13,* No.1 (1959): 51-54.

3. David Peretz, "Reaction to Loss," in *Loss and Grief: Psychological Management in Medical Practice,* ed. Bernard Schoenberg et al. (New York: Columbia University Press, 1970).

4. The warning of impending death was found to lead to more satisfactory adjustment at the end of a year than did the situations in which there was no warning. Anticipation allows some preparation. For example, see Ira Glick et al., *The First Year of Bereavement* (New York: John Wiley & Sons, 1974); Colin Murray Parkes, *Bereavement: Studies of Grief in Adult Life.*

5. William Niederland, "The Survivor Syndrome: Further Observations and Dimensions," *Journal of the American Psychoanalytic Association, 29,* No.2 (1981): 413-426.

6. Ira Glick et al., *The First Year.*

7. Martha Wolfenstein, *Disaster: A Psychological Essay* (Glencoe, IL: Free Press, 1957).

8. James L. McGough, "Hormonal Influences on Memory Storage," *American Psychologist,* 38, No.2 (February, 1983): 161-173.

9. George Krupp, "The Bereavement Reactions," in *Psychoanalytic Study of Society,* Vol.2 (New York: International Universities Press, 1962).

10. Karl Stern, Gwendolyn M. Williams, and Miguel Pardos, "Grief Reactions in Later Life," *American Journal of Psychiatry, 108* (1951): 289-294.

11. George Pollock, "Mourning and Adaptation"; David Peretz, "Reactions to Loss"; Colin Murray Parkes, *Studies of Grief.*

12. Robert J. Lifton, *The Broken Connection,* p. 189.

13. George Krupp, "The Bereavement Reaction."

six

Reorganization

At the beginning of this book, mourning was described as a process in which an individual, confronted with the loss of something or someone significant, undergoes a series of stages that decathect the previous attachment, allowing separation and eventual reinvestment in modified relationships, roles, or ideals. This statement is deceptively simple. After following these women through painful years of their lives, it becomes apparent that the process is very complex.

A somewhat different definition of mourning has evolved from this work: Mourning is the survivor's struggle to let go of that which is already gone. The physical, living world containing the child must be relinquished, while memories, spirit, and representations of the loved person are integrated into a changed, ongoing life. The modified equilibrium which is established allows an alliance with the past and a life in the present.

The entire process is one of adaptation, a continuous striving toward acceptable compromise with life, neither total triumph over the environment nor total surrender to it. Previous chapters have examined the coping of the early days, weeks, and months. We saw the changes in the nature of the compromises that were made over time. What was adaptive in the early days inhibited development as the struggle to hold on/let go progressed. This chapter continues to follow the patterns of coping during the later stages of mourning—what aspects of the women's lives have been transformed and what changes have been made internally and behaviorally as a result of the continuing struggle.

The women studied were in various stages of the mourning process, from the disorganization still seen at the end of the first year to reorganization, seen most clearly after the third year. The reorganizational levels are examined year by year in an attempt to define the patterns in progression during mourning. Of the women interviewed, three were completing the first year of bereavement, three were in the later portion of the second year, five were in the third, and five were beyond that time. Distinguishing progress by year is artificial. There is no timetable to the process. But it is useful in understanding the shifts that occur. There was a great deal of individual variety, but there were also patterns that allow an examination of the changes, best seen by divisions of time (see Table 4 in the Appendix).

Fortunately, there were over 100 additional responses from questionnaires that asked, "To what extent does grief affect your daily life?" Those responses provided complementary data from a larger number of women than the ones interviewed.

STARTING BACK

> I say to myself, 'What did I used to think about? What used to be on my mind previous to when Larry died?' Now that is what takes up my whole spare time. I haven't been able to get it out of my system.
>
> (Louise)

Frances, Deborah, and Anne were three women who were just at the first anniversary of the child's death. Deborah and Anne had many questions and unresolved emotions at the close of the first year, while Frances was determined to "accept" without too many questions. These two styles were related to the individual personality, not to the length of time since the death or the relationship to the child, and were seen at other points in the mourning process.

By the end of the first year, most physical symptoms had disappeared. Bouts of depression continued but there was a return to daily activities, although functioning was intermittently impaired, particularly in decision making or in events that triggered associations to the death. Frances and Anne had gone back to work but Anne said that her career in antiques, tied to her daughter's interest in the same area, "was now my greatest pain." Deborah had done little work in advertising during the year for the same reason. Both daughters were closely identified with the mothers and their career choices, making work extremely difficult. Both Anne and Deborah had work in which their daughters took part. They had dreams of a shared future which had to be abandoned. The pleasure in pursuing that aspect of their lives was gone because of the essential part played by the child.

Deborah was beginning to address ways of making aspects of her career more satisfying by altruistic activities. For example, she was developing a plan to work with sick children doing puppet shows or telling stories, "Sort of like Salinger's *Catcher in the Rye,* the guy that's going to stand on the edge of the field and keep them all from falling off the cliff." This would be an activity allowing her to use her special talents in a way closely related to the importance of the child. Frances, too, expressed the satisfaction she received from helping others, saying she was happiest then.

These women were conscious of their dependency needs, of the help they got from being helpful, and made active attempts to strike a balance between leaning on friends and family without becoming burdensome. All three were still very sensitive and affect, particularly crying, came easily.

They said that they were changed, more sensitive to others and more understanding of loss and tolerant of idiosyncratic coping. What did they see for themselves in the future? Anne said that suicide was a real possibility for her, especially because it was an acceptable answer in her family. The only thing preventing it was the damage it would do to her remaining children. Deborah and Frances thought they would get "a little tougher" or "a little stronger," but at the present time, the pain at each thought that the child was dead was "just as great as the first time."

The coping styles of Frances and Deborah differed, but both had realistic hopes for the future and sublimatory activities and supports which indicate a better chance for their long-term adaptation.

The major pattern in questionnaire responses supports the description of the ever-present nature of the loss during this year. The 28 women (22.4 percent) who were in the first year of mourning wrote frequently that "It's always there." For many of them, the outstanding dynamic of this year is the frequency with which they think about the child and events surrounding the death. "I think of her 100 times a day with a deep sense of longing," and thoughts appear to encompass the pregnancy and delivery, if it was an early death. They also note the reminders such as holidays, other children, and specific precipitators that touch sensitively on the loss. The responses were primarily marked by frequency of thoughts and daily reminders.

LOOKING FOR NEW DIRECTIONS

> They say after two years it makes a difference. I don't think so . . . what has occurred is as real now as it was then.
>
> (Julia)

Mandy, Louise, and Marion were in the last few months of the second year of bereavement. The women interviewed had a great deal in common: good relationships with their late adolescent sons, similar questioning attitudes about their experience, and a search for meaning. The women were still grieving for their children and the pain of the loss continued to surface but was more integrated with life activities.

Marion had joined a bereaved parents self-help group and moved from being helped to actively helping others, assuming leadership in that organization. Louise, too, had joined a different chapter of that group and was engaged in administrative work but continued to benefit from the help she received from other members. She had, in the past year, taken an interest in a quadriplegic young man and was helping him adjust to his accident. She analyzed the relationship as

> I can do for him what I wasn't able to do with my son . . . . This kid is going to need help the rest of his life . . . . He is giving me something physical to put this longing to. I am trying to reach out and do something but I don't know what. Once I found him, I am able to do a little for him, but it helps me out a whole lot.

He will never get well and leave her. Louise had discussed at length her desire to have been able to "do something" for her son and the frustration at her inability to do anything in that instance. Now she has found a use for the "leftover mothering."

Mandy was still searching. She said,

> I feel . . . that there is someone out in this world that I could help immensely with my tragedy, but as of yet, I have not, I feel I have not met that person.

This is one form that the legacy of losing a child can take. The women are searching, often in maternal or nurturing ways, for someone to help, still, in part, to help themselves. These particular women were not responding with career modifications, partly because their jobs were not central to their identities. They looked for ways that complemented their maternal identification and were closely related to the death of a child. In seeing the directions that adaptation takes, it is remarkable how closely integrated it becomes with mothering.

These women, too, see changes in themselves. Mandy said that now "everybody" means a husband and two sons, not three. Louise said that it was easier than the year before. They all said that they were able to go out but sometimes found it hard to be with strangers and preferred the company of family and close friends.

> I feel like they can just look at me. It is like they are staring at me because I feel so bad inside. I almost feel like a cripple. Sometimes out in public I want to say that. Sometimes shopping in the store, I feel like everybody can just see how bad I really feel. Yet they can't. But, yet they can.
>
> (Louise)

They were also beginning to deal with having fun again and questioned whether the return of pleasure was being disloyal to the dead child or forgetting him. Feeling pleasure can precipitate guilt feelings because it makes the mother wonder if she will lose all feeling and memories of the child.

The 39 women in the second year (31.2 percent) showed a greater variety of responses than those of the first year. The same evocative stimuli were noted but more mention was made of lingering symptoms such as nightmares, fears, depression, lack of motivation, and difficulty going back out into the world. The physical aspects of daily functioning seem to have returned to normal but the emotional effects persist. "There is not a day when I don't think of Timmy. I don't cry every day—rather I build up to it over a period of time," captures both the presentness of thoughts and the time in between. The frequency with which women mention lingering symptoms may be due to surprise as they come to grips with the duration of the process and its intensity. Combining these responses with interview data, it becomes clear that they expected it "to get better" more quickly. Symptoms are mentioned frequently in the second year because they continue longer than expected This year brings more of a realization of enduring loss with a physical and emotional toll—acceptance comes to mean irrevocable change.

ACCEPTANCE

> I know I'm a survivor now. I didn't know that before, not before Lynn.
>
> (Marcia)

The women in the third year of bereavement were Julia, Jane, Sherry, Marcia, and Sandy. By this time, the intense rawness of earlier days is gone and personal coping styles are firmly in place, very adaptively for some. But for those women who had a common sense, rational approach to life, it was difficult to go back and discuss the death.

They accepted the loss in different ways. Sherry's daughter was killed in an accident with other neighborhood girls, so there was community mourning and support, facilitating adjustment. Julia and Sherry had unshakable faith in God's will so personal questioning, if it had gone on earlier, was resolved.

> I had faith then, I have faith now. And frankly did lose it or question too much. I was lucky to have children to begin with . . . I kept in mind that we had him this long.
>
> (Julia)

Not all women have this attitude, but many of them said, in different ways,

> Nothing to do except pick up the pieces . . . and realize that life does not go on forever.

It is especially useful to have questionnaire responses from this period. The comments from the 24 women in the third year relate to the interview theme of "going on" and integrating the loss with life activities. There was mention of few symptomatic reactions, but thoughts of the child continue. Responses tended to agree with the woman who wrote "I think my 'good days' far exceed my 'bad days' at this point."

Another noted that "I *live* with this grief, but living now, not just surviving." There is some mention, too, of changed priorities and more compassion, but this theme is just beginning to appear.

INTEGRATION

> Part of the legacy . . . is you have to rework your whole goddamn expectations in life . . . and come back to some kind of meaning because it seems so meaningless.
>
> (Lydia)

The final groups of women to be followed in adaptation are those whose children died more than three years prior to the interview. This was a fascinating group of five: Betty, Sylvia, Thelma, Lydia, and Patty. Through them, some of the milestones of growth in the paths they took since the time of the death can be traced.

Patty had become involved in Compassionate Friends after the first year in an attempt to give a purpose to a life "which I felt was worthless." She worked with other bereaved parents, first partly to help herself, then because the work gave her "self-satisfaction" but not "emotional help." She has recently moved toward helping other bereaved parents take over as the direct helpers, another step away. Now, after six years, she is advising hospitals on working with grieving people. In four years, we can see similarities in Lydia's progress. She is a clinical specialist, doing therapy with grieving adults and also working with behaviorally disordered children. About the work with children, she says, "I couldn't save her (the daughter); maybe I can save someone else." Work in this area is a way that Lydia continues to grieve:

> In this culture, it's difficult after the first few months to keep grieving . . . I found a way to do that legitimately.

From the grief work, then, she gets what Patty would call "emotional help," the ability to continue to pursue her own needs as well as to help others. It enables her to pursue deeper levels of acceptance of the loss.

Lydia also talked about the need to do something "creative," an idea raised by many theorists and articulated frequently by Pollock, who notes that the vulnerability from the encounter with death gives rise, in some, to pathology. But others demonstrate new directions of mastery and creativity. Lifton, too, notes creativity in discussing men and women who have made a successful transition into middle age. He finds that the basic developmental task of that period, confrontation with one's own mortality, has risks, but the "increased capacity to imagine the end of the self can release powerful, revitalizing energies—if one can relate that image to the questioning of ultimate choices and of the quality of immediate experience."[1] In their individual ways, these women are expressing the need to create, to see life reborn from the destruction.

Betty, too, was involved with Compassionate Friends, helping others. She saw her role there as reversing over time, first getting help and then giving it. In her case, any direction she might have pursued that was directly related to the death was altered by present problems. Her husband was diagnosed with lymphoma three years ago and his health has declined, absorbing more and more of her time and attention. They have turned to a self-help group for people with life-threatening illness and are becoming active there. It brings us to another aspect of adaptation. Patty said that some of the work is learning "to live again," meaning the ability to deal with present problems, and the possibility of more losses. The idea of learning to live again is illustrated in Patty's experience where, two years after her daughter's death, her other daughter collapsed and stopped breathing. She froze and saw her dead daughter lying on the floor instead. The next year her father died, and she was able to respond to her family's needs, but, more importantly to her, she felt that she grieved for him, not for the child, and was no longer confused about whom she was responding to.

It is an interesting progression. We see vividly how loss tends to awaken the fear of future loss; how present losses reactivate feelings connected to past losses; and now, how loss can finally be addressed for the meaning of that event only.

Living again does not only mean the capacity to respond to new losses.It is also the capacity to respond to pleasure. Sylvia said the hurt keeps getting duller and "further away." Lydia and Thelma had referred to "double guilt"—first the guilt at losing the child and then the guilt at experiencing relief that a conflictual relationship has ended. Adaptation also brings a "double loss."

> First you lose the child, then you lose the pain from losing the child.
>
> (Patty)

That is the price of adjustment. At first these women looked forward to the day when they would feel less pain, less emotional absorption with the death. When the day comes, it can be experienced as another loss. There is some guilt in finally being able to go on, to live, to retain the memories of the child but "not as a growing, living, breathing part" of the family.

As the good days far outnumber the bad ones, infrequent periods of sadness can be enjoyed, even treasured, as the last emotional connections with the child.

> I couldn't wait until I healed enough so that I could go on, and when I did, it felt funny, real strange . . . There's this whole thing about somehow the depth of my grief is some measure of my caring for her, and that to let go of that means I don't care . . . so that's another thing you have to struggle with.
>
> (Lydia)

The 15 (12 percent) questionnaire responses from the fourth and fifth years become more diverse. Some women note the daily sense of loss accompanied by healing, others say that the grief is "not always painful," and others report little affect any longer. The diversity itself is an important trend and it shows that individual personality and lifestyles have differentiated the women at this point, whereas previously the intensity of the internal experience brought out similarities.

The 19 women who lost children more than five years before said that they were changed. They described changes in values, priorities, self-concept, and mothering. A few mentioned that they have begun to help others who are grieving. The loss does not disappear. A woman in Colorado wrote,

> Yesterday while cleaning a pan I thought of Sean. Six years—I haven't seen him for six years! His smiling face still so clear it hurts. It has lessened but still affects all facets of life.

At this point, the women appear to have reached an adjustment and acceptance of the loss as an unchangeable part of their lives.

This is where we leave these women in the mourning process—engaged again in satisfying life activities often related to the child's death, which was one of the most profound experiences in their lives. They appear to have incorporated the experience into their ongoing lives, having learned that adaptation does not mean going back to the way things were, but rather compromising with the way things are and will be. This last group struggles again to "let go": this time of the absorption and the pain in favor of living.

> The image is of her by some kind of water, in the grass, under a tree, and she's just sitting there waiting . . . . My sense is that it has something to do with my letting her go . . . and this year I told her she could go, and she got up and started to walk away, and I said, "No, wait, give me one more year. I can't let you go yet." And she came back.
>
> (Lydia)

NOTE

1. George Pollock, "On Mourning, Immortality, and Utopia," *Journal of the American Psychoanalytic Association, 23,* No.2 (1975): 334-362; Robert Lifton, *The Broken Connection,* p. 88.

Part Two

seven

Emotional and Social Supports: Family and Friends

In Part One, the focus was on the individual woman and her bereavement experience. However, she is not alone during the years of mourning. She interacts daily with others. In this chapter we look at the dynamics of some of these very important relationships: who was helpful, how and why they were, and some of the changes that occurred in relationships during the bereavement period.

The emphasis again is on the woman's experience, reported in interviews and questionnaires, as they describe what happened with husbands, children, family members, and friends—some of their deepest relationships. The love, comfort, and pain in these interactions are powerful forces in adaptation to loss.

Social support is defined as information leading an individual to believe she is cared for and loved, and/or esteemed and valued, and/or a member of a network of mutual obligations.[1] This definition implies that an institution providing service is not in itself support, although the attitudes of staff may be supportive. Social support, defined as information, becomes immeasurable in terms of mass or energy but is clearly tied to the recipient's perception.

Research continues to support the notion that "good" social supports influence physical and emotional well-being.[2] Unfortunately, the attempts to objectively measure whether or not social supports are high have had to make certain assumptions as to the criteria about what constitutes "good" social supports. For example, assuming marriage or specialized medical care as an indicator of social support negates the individual perception and experience of that particular relationship and what is communicated. Ultimately, it is the individual's perception of the relationship that affects her emotional and behavioral responses. It has been speculated that women may have an advantage over men in supports because of a greater sensitivity to close relationships and greater versatility in choice of objects for such relationships.

In studying the parents who had experienced the death of a child, Lieberman identified "primary helpers" because the parents had multiple use of resources. He concluded that in situations of extreme loss, the overall amount of help did not buffer the individual from the psychological consequences of stress, but the crucial factor was *who* provided the help. In this instance, the help of the spouse was central.[3]

THE MARRIAGE

> My husband never mentioned her name for two years. They both played the piano. He won't touch it now.
>
> (Sylvia)

> I guess instinctively we realized that this is so big and overwhelming that if we can't communicate with each other through it, we won't make it.
>
> (Marion)

The death of a child rips through the family, subjecting individuals and the relationships among them to enormous stress. It is seen poignantly in the marriage. Both have suffered the death of their child, but the shared nature of the loss can work against the couple. Intense grief is an isolating experience.

In their view, the husbands had less daily contact with the child, and therefore fewer daily reminders of the loss. But the men were the primary wage earners in these families and returned to work shortly after the death so the emptiness in the house hit them when they came home in the evenings. Their stress was compounded by interactions with business associates and friends who did not know about the death or, if they knew, were unable to express sympathy and offer comfort. These encounters resulted in the men spending their time at home emotionally drained and depressed.

A number of women referred to the "balance" in their relationships with their husbands. If he cried, she showed less affect; if he did not acknowledge the loss, she reacted more intensely. These were marriages of long standing. The partners had worked out an emotional equilibrium over the years. Some marriages continued as they were, but the stress of the event caused other marriages to undergo changes. The couple found new ways of behaving in order to adjust to the loss. The dynamic of "balance" offered the possibility of strengthening of weakening the marriage. Some maintained the old ways, but temporarily became more extreme. Several reversed traditional behaviors. For example, Louise, the extroverted wife, became shy and her husband increased in his gregariousness. Others modified the relationship, working out new compromises that facilitated adaptation.

Previously, the individual mourning process was discussed as a process of reestablishing a modified equilibrium based on the changed reality. Here it is seen that this struggle also extends to primary relationships.

During the time the husbands and wives spent together, each was absorbed by individual mourning. At times it caused an inability to attend to, comfort, or empathize with the other. Trauma tends to bring out different reactions. Wives often said that they expressed their grief differently from their husbands. Women noted that the men were more concerned with a show of strength. They had trouble talking about the death or their feelings after the initial impact. The women were more expressive and had a strong need to discuss the death.

Most women felt that they were the primary caregivers in relation to the children, had more interaction with them, and were therefore more exposed to daily reminders. But they also said that there were more people who were willing and able to provide comfort, support, and help with many tasks, mitigating the stress. They said that people responded more easily to the mother's loss than to the father's. His grief was less noticed.

The husband and wife must cope with the loss individually and as a couple. Dyadic styles and equilibrium that had been useful in the past often became a hindrance to one or both of them after the death. The greatest difficulty arose from the inability to discuss how they felt and what to do about decisions related to the loss. For example, keeping the child's possessions or giving them away, visiting the cemetery, beliefs about an afterlife, behavior in public, and pleasure of all kinds, including sexual, were issues that needed continued attention, and brought out different feelings and ideas in men and women.

When the two were unable to talk, the needed compromises were impossible and resentments grew. Things said and done remained unforgivable. For most of the women interviewed, marital compromises were worked out and they established areas of give and take, sometimes doing things together and sometimes apart. If the husband wanted to visit the cemetery weekly, the wife had breakfast waiting at home; if the wife was unable to care for the remaining children, the husband stepped in; if making dinner became impossible, they went out; or if the husband could not face the world after a day at work, they curtailed social activities in the evenings. Sometimes, if they could not compromise, they learned to tolerate the areas of disagreement. Not all of the grief could be shared, even in marriages that were stable and gratifying, and where loss was experienced as shared. Much of the coping within the marital dyad was tolerating the separateness of the other and the loneliness of the experience without becoming permanently estranged. In those relationships where the balance was struck between sharing and being alone, the women felt that they weathered the experience well.

> About two weeks after the funeral, when the food was gone, I had said to Ted, "What do you feel like having for dinner tonight? He said, "Maybe we should have some fish." So I got in the car and went to the store and they didn't have any. Of course, right next to the fish counter is the whole meat department, but they didn't have any fish and I wasn't about to make up my mind what else I was going to have. So I turned right around and walked out of the store and I went home. I said to Ted, "Well they didn't have any fish so I guess that we are going to have to go out." He said, "Fine." We did. He didn't say to me, "Didn't they have anything else?" He just said okay.
>
> (Marcia)

Most marriages returned to stability after the upheaval and several women expressed pride in the way that they "got through it together." They said their marriages were stronger.

The shared loss can also reveal deeper levels of understanding and compassion because the child belonged to both, and mothers often felt that no one could understand the loss as completely as her husband. The child had been part of their bond and history together. Most marriages have both dynamics—both separation and unification in grief.

There were certain patterns in the women's perceptions of their marriages and the women who responded to questionnaires substantiated these interviews (Table 8 in Appendix). Husbands were very important as sources of support and women tended to turn to them before anyone else or not at all, but whatever his significance before the child's death it was strongly indicative of his importance after the first year. For most women, there was no change at all. If a change occurred, it was during that difficult first year, when the temporary, but painful and isolating conflicts were strongest. It appears that the balance in the marriages was upset by the trauma and required tolerance and compromise to help the couple's adaptation to the loss.

RELATIONSHIPS WITH CHILDREN

> I absolutely made it miserable for him to be gone. Where are you going to go? Who are you going with? I was panicky about him being in a car.
>
> (Marcia)

The relationship between the mothers and their remaining children are deeply affected by the death. Each must cope with changes in other family members as well as their own reactions.

Children who lived at home were exposed to the family's full grief, a very powerful experience. But these children also had people available to them who shared the tragedy and that often had a healing effect. Children living away from home had other interests to divert their attention but missed being close to the family and others who knew their sister or brother.

Younger children often showed an identification with their dead sister or brother. Patty's daughter "became just like her for a year," and Betty's son has turned into a "tough guy," following his brother's behaviors:

> His brother was so much bigger.It was like hero-worship. He just thinks Luke was the biggest, toughest, not the goodest, maybe even the baddest guy, and so, that's what he's trying to emulate. He wants to be like Luke was.
>
> (Betty)

These children responded to the empty place in the family by trying to fill it. Their burden was not only to fill the gap in the family, but also to stay safe and not worry their parents any further.

> Well, just when we're all grieving at our most difficult, intense level (my son) started showing a lot of anger . . . and he started using it toward us which, we were so devastated emotionally anyhow, and all of a sudden we have this, our only son, turn on us.
>
> (My therapist) said, "You'd never failed him before as parents and he's, among other things, angry that somehow you hadn't taken better care of her." . . . And the other thing was that he didn't want to have to be good or be safe just because we've lost her . . . .
>
> We can't hide the caring, but we, we can bite our tongues once in a while.
>
> (Deborah)

Even the children could gratify the parents with safety and successes, the milestones that these remaining children reached only reminded them all, once again, of the future denied to the dead sibling. When these children moved past their siblings in age or achievements, they experienced guilt for receiving what was denied the other.

Some remaining children experienced problems that the mothers believed were caused or exacerbated by the death. They were subject to depression, nightmares, terrible loneliness, and sometimes guilt for fights and bad feelings. They were often angry and overwhelmed. Mandy was not the only one who bought her son a puppy. It took his attention, energy and love. "He had to help raise her. It helped him through a bad time." Several children went into therapy, one was feared to be suicidal. Other children withdrew from activities and social relationships. In some instances school was missed and grades suffered. Remaining children were often subjected to insensitive comments from classmates and people in the community. The parents' terror mounted with any additional problems from other children. These problems increased the parents' fears of future loss.

> I saw Mark (age 16) having more and more difficulties with being able to stay at school. More and more trouble sleeping. The depression getting so intense . . . . And then he left . . . just thinking that he could run from his misery . . . . At one time he said, 'I thought that if I died the pain would go away.'
>
> . . . I was terrified. I guess Ted and I got so worried about what he might do and we felt so totally helpless. We knew. We tried to help

him. And we couldn't. So we were frustrated in that way. We tried to protect him. We tried to take the pain away.

(Marcia)

Women spoke differently about remaining sons and daughters, young children and older ones. Some mothers had tried to shield the younger children from the details of the death and the decisions that had to be made; the result often was that the child felt alone and left out.

The ability to mourn has its own line of development, beginning in early life and reaching maturity after adolescence when the psychic apparatus is fully developed. Although Bowlby notes that children mourn during separations from or loss of their parents, most others have maintained that childhood mourning, and even the mourning process inherent in adolescent detachment from parents, is only a forerunner to mature adult mourning.[4]

Very briefly, young children, under the age of two, react to the change in the parents' behavior, not directly to the death of their sibling. By three years old, children have more of an understanding of death, often gained from having pets. Also, at this time, the children are developing rich fantasy lives and may distort much of what they hear about death. By the age of seven, they are more reality oriented but their feelings are more muted than previously. It is with adolescence that mourning begins to take forms similar to the process in adulthood.

Many mothers, those interviewed and questionnaire respondents, said that remaining children had become more important to them—more precious. But when women turned to their children for help and emotional support, it was usually to their daughters. The daughters were important for two different reasons. The young girls, under ten years old, still needed a mother's care and the women found that was gratifying. The more mature daughters, 18 years and older, were singled out as companions for the mothers. Women felt that they talked more with daughters. The daughters mourned like their mothers, expressing grief openly and wanting to talk about the child. The similarities provided mutual support (see Table 6 in Appendix).

They described their sons as grieving privately or withdrawing, with occasional episodes of acting out behavior. The sons' grief was often similar to depictions of the husbands' bereavement. It seems that the gender differences in style, emotional display, and behavior is very real, and, for a time at least, can widen the gulf between family members (see Table 7 in Appendix).

The changes brought by time take the dead child away from the family. Because he or she is locked into the past, every step taken by the living is a reminder of what cannot be. Every change made by family members brings them further away from the time when the lost child had a physical presence in the family.

RELATIONSHIPS WITH OTHER FAMILY MEMBERS

> I had not cried until my mother opened the door . . . and I just sobbed like a little two-year-old in her arms and I don't ever remember doing that before in my life.
>
> (Mandy)

Relationships with other family members generally remain remarkably stable. For those women who relied on their families of origin it was, in part, because they lived nearby, shared a common past with the mother which provided a strong sense of security and continuity, and loved the child. The loss was very much shared (see Table 8 in Appendix).

But, in many instances, by the middle years, a woman's parents are often dead, aging, or ill, so dependency may be reversed. Sisters and brothers often live far away. Family members, although they offer empathy and support, are not always available on a daily basis. By midlife a woman's identification and allegiance has shifted to her own family.

Younger women, more often than older ones, tended to depend on family members, especially mothers. It was the women ranging in age from 22 to 34 years at the time of the death who reported relying most on their mothers. Often these women had no other children. The child who died was to have been the first. In a study of mothers who had stillborns it was found that, in those cases where they could not talk openly with their husbands, the women confided their thoughts and feelings to their mothers. Again this was a group of younger mothers.[5]

A picture of family relationships begins to emerge. The husband is central as a support. But some marriages feel the stress strongly and may be strained, either permanently or temporarily. One aspect of the estrangement is the isolating effects of grief, separating the husband and wife. It appears that women move from the closeness with their own mother, become the mother, and grow closer to their own daughters. The shift in the middle years is to a reliance on one's created family, made all the more important by one child's death. The woman's family of origin recedes in daily importance, but remains as a symbol of stability, reassurance, and security in the midst of traumatic change.

RELATIONSHIPS WITH FRIENDS

> My friend Carol is usually there when I need a friend to listen.
>
> (Sandy)

Friends were very important to the women during their mourning. They were available emotionally and in daily contact with the mother, providing comfort and help. Women tended to have at least one good woman friend to talk to and to depend on, and most had several with whom she felt comfortable. Friends were there to help with shopping, children, decisions, or just to sit and have coffee. Good friends were needed for a long time and valued highly. Most women had a special friend, almost always another woman and usually slightly older. Few had good men friends, and those were work supervisors or husbands of close women friends. Mostly, a reliance on other women was noted.

All the women studied had many casual friends and acquaintances, and it was with this second group that the women experienced discomfort. Most said they were careful about what feelings or thoughts they revealed. They did not want to burden or alienate others and were sensitive about displaying too much emotion. They were very aware of other people's reactions to them and the theme of "fear of contagion" emerged from these descriptions.

> I think it has been frightening to some of our friends and relatives who think if it happened to us, it can happen to them.
>
> (Sylvia)

> I got the distinct impression that there were those people who kind of avoided us.
>
> (Sylvia's husband)

Friends, acquaintances, coworkers, and some family members avoided these women. It appears that people stay away for two reasons.

One, they do not know what to say that will be "correct" and fear reminding the woman of the tragedy. Two, they do not want to be reminded that it could happen to them and they, too, would be helpless to prevent it. Louise thought it was her imagination when she saw a friend quickly head down a different aisle in the grocery store, and Mandy assumed that a young man who ignored her had just forgotten that they knew one another. Deborah found that the mothers of her daughter's friends just stopped calling her. All women experienced conversations that included everything but the topic that was most on her mind, the child's death.

The conversations that avoided the child were particularly painful to these women. Not talking about the child meant, to them, that they were pretending the child never existed and everything was unchanged. Talking about the child was a strong need, but they were sensitive about forcing the topic on others. The child lives on through his or her family, so to avoid the name was denying the past existence and thwarting the possibility of future.

Family and friends were equally sensitive and did not want to remind the mother of the tragedy, which, Louise said, ". . . is silly. It's there, they could never remind me of it."

Some of the self-consciousness is because there is not much that other people can say. The mothers hated the platitudes, easy reassurances, or casual equations with other losses. These women believed that no one could really know what they were going through, except those who had experienced the same loss. But they needed and were grateful for the contact with people, the opportunities to talk about the child, and inquiries into their own well-being.

The question of who is being protected by avoiding the mother or the subject of the child's death is an important one. It appears likely that friends and family were also protecting themselves. It was as if they could "catch the disease" by getting close. The unexpected death of a child engenders fear in people. Seeing it happen to a friend reminds everyone else that they would like immunity from such a tragedy. It is also likely that guilt is a component of these reactions. After all, there is the triumph of not being the one hit by tragedy—perhaps one's own family is safe.

The event makes others uncomfortable, embarrassed by their own internal responses, and what is *not* said becomes the underlying focal point of the interaction. The helplessness of the friends are two-fold: the inability to do anything for the mother, and the inability to protect themselves.

The helplessness in confronting accidental and unexpected death has been a powerful dynamic in the mother's bereavement. Friends defend against helplessness, too. In some cases, their actions hurt the women's feelings. It is well illustrated by an incident that occurred to Louise when she returned to work.

> This one girl that I work with, her son did a stupid thing and cut his leg . . . and was laid up for a long time. I'll bet you I heard that story a hundred times . . . . Everybody that saw her (said), "How's Tim doing?" She was able to say that he is progressing . . . . She'd go through the whole story . . . . It is something that can be healed, so they are not afraid of it.

Women responded to these interactions in several ways. Sometimes they would be hurt, angry, and withdraw from the person or conversation. But in many cases, they took the initiative to put people at ease and to reestablish relationships. They would seek others out and casually mention the child to let them know it was not a taboo subject. They also tried on many occasions to avoid showing affect to spare other people's discomfort. Some were proud of their "stoicism" and valued their strength as long as they had the time and place to vent their emotions. Bravery in public proved to them that they could "survive" and continue functioning, and there was satisfaction in knowing that. Being brave served another function for some. When they pretended nothing was wrong, people did not probe and they were given some time to be normal. This also reflects the feeling of being different—that something so wrong had happened. Sylvia stopped wearing her name tag at the hospital where she worked so that she could be anonymous some of the time. In this way, she avoided questions, solicitousness, or pity. At times these women resented being throught of as brave, receiving compliments or admiration. Deborah said,

> What is there to do? One doesn't really have any choice I suppose. Go around and kick kids off tricycles because yours is dead? You really don't have any other choice . . . so somehow in people's minds . . . they think, "Oh, they're God-loving, God-fearing people" or something.

They were also afraid of what people would think of them if they appeared "normal" or to be having a good time. If the mother went to a party, laughed or enjoyed herself, she assumed that others would think she had forgotten the child. This relates back to the mother's own struggle about experiencing pleasure and her fears about forgetting the child. Mandy's friend compared her to another bereaved mother and noted that the other mother looked worse. "Was that a compliment? I wondered about it all day."

The stoicism and fears about showing inappropriate affect are partly related to self-esteem, but there is also a deeply felt and widespread belief that display of affect is a sign of weakness, and out of place after the first few weeks of bereavement. The lengthiness of the mourning process surprised the women themselves. People expected the women to be "finished" with grieving and back to normal. It adds to the pressure to behave as if nothing tragic had happened after a relatively short period of time. This causes the mothers and their friends to have an increasingly difficult time if she continues to talk about the child. The women said they needed to continue talking but opportunities to do so diminished as the months passed. The specialness of family and friends who remember the child and continue talking with her is increased by the expectations of others who want her to stop grieving.

The women were also extremely sensitive to innocuous remarks made by friends. Common complaining about children took on additional meaning for the mother who wished that she had a child to complain about. The remarks angered the mother and reawakened the longing for the particular child.

The intolerance extended to other spheres of life as well. Jane noted,

> The normal bullshit in life . . . I don't have any tolerance for it at all . . . . It's because they were trivial to start with and when the chips are down and the absolute worst has happened, what difference does it make what color your shoes are?

Conversely, the women believe that they understand people better. They feel they have more compassion and "don't think I will ever be critical of anyone again. I really think that whatever gets people through life, if you don't hurt anyone, there is no right and there is no wrong." This comes, in part, from their own belief that they never could have been able to predict beforehand what their reactions, feelings, and actions would have been. They develop a deep acceptance of anyone else's grief and idiosyncratic ways of coping with death.

In spite of the difficulties that they experienced with some of their friends, coworkers, or acquaintances, most women were pleasantly surprised by their close friends: "They didn't quit on me." In spite of their intense needs, particularly during the first year, the women who were past that period look back and say they received a great deal of support.

Friends gained markedly in importance during that first year following the death, but some dropped significantly after that time (see Table 9 in the Appendix) to whatever their importance had been before the death. This is explained by the need for multiple resources to help get through the first year. Some of the friends were people associated with the tragedy, making them significant but temporary relationships. If the primary link was the child's death, it is expected that as adaptation progresses, these friendships must change or become transitional in nature. Other people drift away. The women noted that others do not like to be around a grieving mother. Some relationships endure through the intense mourning and afterward. Many women said that although they were not presently close to all the same people, those that helped them through the difficult period remain special.

CHARACTERISTICS OF SUPPORTIVE INDIVIDUALS

> There were three of us that go to Church . . . and we'd get together and have coffee afterward. We didn't always talk about this situation, you know, but we could talk about anything.
>
> (Sherry)

It has been seen that these women have many resources in family members and friends. Much support is available. What is it then, that makes certain people more important to them than others? Women responded with consistency about what they valued in these relationships, often using identical words to describe significant people. The individuals who were experienced as being most helpful were those who possessed one or more of the following characteristics: they shared the experience of the child's death; they were available and not withdrawn; they had been through a similar experience; they forced the mourner to go on with her life; or they performed specific tasks for the mother.

Shared experience included those people, particularly husbands and family members, who had loved the child, suffered the loss, and could remember the child with the mother. These people not only shared the present pain but also the past joys. Both could be relived together. The descriptions of these people conveyed the quality of mutuality—of the care and love of the child and similar feelings about the death. These people were often those who were important in the mother's past, who had known her before the tragedy and loved her. The change is great in the mother's life, so to have been known "before" is very important. The word "shared" was often used to describe past and present joys and sorrow, and love for one another and the child.

Available and not withdrawn described those people who were "not afraid of me" and who "allowed" endless talking without "feeling uncomfortable." These people were the ones who could tolerate the mother's pain without withdrawing. Sometimes it meant just listening. It was not an active response, but one of "being there," listening and understanding. The word "allowed" was an interesting choice and appears to mean the opposite of withdrawing, evaluating, or judging her worlds, feelings, or actions. It was used frequently, and suggested that women experienced others as uncomfortable, and unable to tolerate the pain.

Women felt tainted by their closeness to death. People who remained available and allowed them to experience the range of emotions were those who could tolerate their own discomfort as well as her pain. They gave her the freedom to experience the event without messages suggesting that she "get over it." Their availability also conveyed to the mother that her feelings and her experiences were legitimate and she was valued.

Having been through a similar experence was a lesser theme. Some specifically referred to another person who had also lost a child and could understand the experience. The women felt intuitively understood by these individuals, even when they were strangers, because they had "been through it." They often felt that others could not understand the experience. Close personal relationships with other bereaved mothers countered some of the isolation. These other mothers were perceived as "knowing" without having to be told. This theme came up again when women spoke about the helpfulness of a self-help group for bereaved parents and was a major dynamic in that experience.

Forcing the mourner to go on living was another lesser theme. The people who were important for this reason were usually their remaining young children. "It gave me a purpose to keep going; I had the children to care for."

The children also provided the mother with proof that she could master some aspects of her life, continue to function and fulfill necessary responsibilities. Most of the women in the interview sample had completed early mothering. Some had no children at home. Others had teenagers who did not want undue care and attention. These middle-years women were denied that opportunity for mastery and repair through remaining children. The theme of fighting the helplessness, woven throughout this study, appears again. The opportunities for "another change" are denied most women in their middle years, forcing them to struggle against the helplessness in other ways.

Having performed specific tasks referred to doctors who gave medical care, professionals who gave advice, and family or friends who brought food, babysat, and arranged funeral services. These people took over some function that the woman was unable to perform at the time. This theme was minor, and usually mentioned in conjunction with other people who helped in more significant ways. Overwhelmingly, the important people were those who provided emotional rather than functional support. Even specific tasks carried the meaning of being cared for and understood.

In spite of the perception of isolation, we see that there are people around who care for, value, and love the woman. She does receive support, even if it does not meet the overwhelming needs of that time. Trauma of this magnitude often requires additional forms of support to facilitate healthy adaptation. In the next chapter we look at professional resources such as clergy, doctors, therapists, and support groups, who are also useful during bereavement.

NOTES

1. Sidney Cobb, "Social Support as a Moderator of Life Stress," *Psychosomatic Medicine, 30,* No.5 (1976): 300-313.

2. Sidney Cobb, "A Model for Life Events and Their Consequences," in *Stressful Life Events: Their Nature and Effects,* ed. B.S. Dohrenwend and B.P. Dohrenwend (New York: John Wiley & Sons, 1974); Katherine Nuckolls, John Cassel, and Berton Kaplan, "Psychosocial Assets, Life Crises, and the Prognosis of Pregnancy," *American Journal of Epidemiology, 95* (1972): 431-441; Jerome Myers, Jacob Lindenthal, and Max Pepper, "Life Events, Social Integration and Psychiatric Symptomatology," *Journal of Health and Social Behavior, 16* (1975): 421-431.

3. Morton Lieberman, "The Effects of Social Supports on Response to Stress."

4. John Bowlby, "Process of Mourning," *International Journal of Psychoanalysis, 42* (1961): 317-340; Martha Wolfenstein,"How Is Mourning Possible?"; Jeanne Lampl-de Groot, "On Adolescence," *Psychoanalytic Study of the Child, 13* (1960): 95-103; Anna Freud, "Adolescence."

5. John H. Kennel, Howard Slyter and Marshall Klaus, "The Mourning Response of Parents to the Death of a Newborn Infant," *New England Journal of Medicine, 283,* no.7 (1970): 344-349.

eight

Social and Emotional Supports: Professionals and a Self-help Group

The past pages have described and explained the mourning process as universal, normal, and essential in detaching from the loss and reinvesting in satisfying activities. We looked at the dynamics of women's bereavement and then at their experience with family and friends. But it is clear that women need multiple resources. A total of 91 women, over 77 percent, reported also turning to professionals—doctors, clergy, therapists—or self-help groups for additional help in coping with the child's death. Almost 53 percent used more than one professional resource (see Table 10 in the Appendix).

This chapter discusses the importance of these people during the bereavement. The concentration is on the psychological resources, different ideas about intervention with bereaved individuals, and the nature of the help.

USE OF PROFESSIONAL RESOURCES

> I went to a social worker after my daughter's death. She helped me grieve and gave me guidance in how to help my family.
>
> (Deborah)

Most women had contact with doctors, clergy, or therapists during mourning, but the results were often unsatisfactory. Interactions with professionals were intensely personalized. Doctors and nurses were often seen not as doing their jobs, but as interfering with the family. Clergy were sometimes dismissed as "not understanding death," or not really knowing the child. Some therapists were experienced as unempathic. On the positive side, many hospital personnel were singled out as helping the family through the nightmare, clergy as providing comfort and answers, and therapists as aiding an understanding of the powerful and overwhelming feelings that tormented some mothers. Professionals were among the first people contacted, but use of these individuals declined after the first year. Thc relationships that were most often maintained were those that had been established before the child's death. In some instances it is easy to see where professional responsibilities or needs clashed with the needs and wishes of the women during their bereavement. They wanted someone to "be there," to listen and to understand. But they also wanted answers and to have their dependency needs met, and in this area, professional help can be less satisfying than that of family and friends.

Increasingly, there have been attempts to ascertain specific information about who uses help, what kinds of help, and for what reasons. A review of the research of those who seek help found that the majority of people who report experiencing stress from a variety of difficult life events do seek help, but help seeking declines consistently with age and is more prevalent among whites than blacks.[1] People who are looking for comfort, reassurance, and advice most commonly combine both social and professional resources, or else exclusively use their friends and family.[2] Women may have an advantage over men because they have greater sensitivity to the importance of forming close relationships and exercise more versatility in their choice of people for those relationships.[3]

Some linkages have been found between certain types of problems and sources of help. The social network appears to be the main source for general worries and unhappiness, with spouses being the primary helpers for worries with friends and the major resource for unhappy emotions. But professional help is sought for problems ranging from severe emotional distress to discrete stress resulting from work or family roles—strains that frequently arise from problems with those generally providing social support.[4]

The three broad categories of professional resources used by the bereaved mothers were doctors, clergy, and therapists, all sought for different reasons. More than 44 percent, or 52 women, noted doctors as important to them. Medical personnel were important before the child died and in the year following, but diminished sharply in significance after that time (see Table 11 in Appendix). The reasons seem to be straightforward: When the child's death was due to an illness, contact with the doctor is essential during the treatment, and in some instances afterward the doctors can help answer questions and console parents. When the doctors had been consulted for problems the women themselves were having, it was during that first year when somatic complaints were at the worst. The problems noted most often for the women were eating and sleep disturbances and depression.

A total of 54 women, 45.8 percent, listed members of the clergy as being important in their lives, especially during the first year after the child's death (see Table 12 in the Appendix). There was a sharp decline in their significance after that first year. The reason for this trend is the tendency to seek out religious resources quickly but to maintain ties in those instances where the predisposition already existed.

Women used psychological resources the least of all professional help. This is explained, in part, by the fact that doctors and clergy were very often a part of the illness and burial process, whereas therapy had to be actively sought by the mother and still conveys, for many, a stigma of mental illness. Only 22 of the women (18.6 percent) noted therapists as important in bereavement. Most of the therapeutic relationships appear to have begun during the first year following the child's death and were very significant then. The drop in importance after that year was equally striking (see Table 13 in the Appendix). Entering treatment was, for some, a direct response to the stress caused by the crisis, and they went for specific reasons rather than for general psychological distress. In those cases, they stopped either in frustration or because needs were met. The therapeutic help included psychiatrists, psychologists, social workers, and grief counselors, and was evenly divided between male and female therapists.

What can be done for a bereaved mother if mourning is normal and necessary? Different researchers have asked some questions about intervention in bereavement. Reviewed here are some studies that specifically address what individuals want or need from therapy; pathological bereavement; and the usefulness of a self-help group for bereaved parents. The programs and theories discussed here address interventions that are directed at facilitating the bereavement process. Therefore, they are generally short-term therapies, with specific goals that focus on the mourning process. It is important to keep in mind that short-term treatment does not imply that bereavement ends in a matter of weeks or months; the mourning continues. Short-term intervention helps that process. It is useful to distinguish short-term focused intervention from more generalized long-term psychotherapy that attempts a greater depth of understanding and working through of this loss and any related issues.

Bereavement intervention studies rarely address grieving parents as a specific group of individuals, so the model for short-term therapy and focused intervention have yet to be satisfactorily demonstrated as effective for child loss. This model does, however, provide helpful conceptualization for bereavement interventions and calls attention to two significant problems: empathic response on the part of the therapist, and stumbling blocks, or risks, in the course of bereavement.

Bereavement Interventions

Alexy questioned whether individuals would need and want different psychological approaches at different stages of the bereavement process, specifically focusing on bereaved parents. He examined the dimensions of action or insight orientation, cognition or conation (strivings, feelings and emotions), and structure or ambiguity during different stages of mourning.[5]

Beginning with the early days of mourning, parents preferred conation to cognition. They wanted a compassionate listener, much as the women of this study described. As the initial numbness wore off, the parents tended toward cognition, especially during the period of searching for their child. The preoccupation with thoughts of the child and a desire to make sense of the event made a cognitive approach more desirable. The cognitive usefulness declines as the parents began to let go of the child and later when they began to reorganize their lives. Ambiguity was preferred over structure during the entire process and Alexy suggested that parents were aware of pressing yet undefined needs which makes structure less responsive to them. During the final stage of bereavement, parents particularly preferred an insight orientation and conation more than action or cognition, suggesting the continuing need to process deep feelings about the loss and adjustment.

One of the more significant aspects of Alexy's work is that he touches on the importance of empathic response to bereaved parents—to their needs and to their changes. Too often, helping professionals equate help with active intervention. If we indeed believe that the process of mourning is necessary and desirable, we must conceptualize therapeutic work as facilitating the process which may mean, for long periods, empathically responding to the helplessness.

Taking a different approach to another important aspects of intervention, Raphael concentrated on the need for preventive programs and attempted to assess and intervene with widows who were likely to be at risk for postbereavement morbidity. A total of 200 widows were questioned during the first weeks after their husbands' deaths.[6] The indicators used to predict risk were those commonly associated with problematic bereavements: high levels of perceived nonsupportiveness; moderate levels of nonsupportiveness with traumatic circumstances surrounding the death; previously highly ambivalent marital relationship, traumatic circumstances, and unmet needs; and concurrent life crisis. Of the 194 retained in the study, 64 were randomly selected for intervention which consisted of selective ego support of relevant bereavement processes, essentially nondirective, although the focus was kept on the mourning process. Specifically, ego support was seen as supporting grieving affects, such as helplessness, hopelessness, sadness, anger, anxiety, and despair. Mourning was also facilitated by reviewing the relationship in both its positive and negative aspects. The average number of sessions was four, although the range was from one through nine. After 13 months, a questionnaire was sent to all groups. The questions focused on health change, as indicated by increased symptomatology, drug or alcohol intake, depression, work capacity, and other variables. The results showed consistent differences. The intervention group showed lessened health impairment when compared with the matched control group who did not receive intervention. Also, they then appeared more like the low-risk group than the other original high-risk group. It appeared that intervention was able to lower individuals from high- to low-risk.

Parkes also notes the preventive potential of therapy during bereavement. In a review of interventions, he concludes that professional

> services and professionally supported voluntary and self-help services are capable of reducing the risk of psychiatric and psychosomatic disorders resulting from bereavement. Services are

> most beneficial among bereaved people who perceive their families as unsupportive or who, for other reasons, are thought to be at special risk (p. 6).[7]

Another study of outcome complicates the picture further. After a rail disaster in Australia in 1977, Raphael attempted to organize a preventive psychiatry outreach program for the relatives of the bereaved and the survivors. Bereavement counseling was offered to all families who were considered to be at risk. A follow-up study was done by Singh and Raphael 15-18 months later to assess the level of functioning of 42 bereaved relatives.[8] Through interviews and questionnaires, they concluded that those with supportive networks tended to do better than those without them; those who received counseling did better than those who did not; those who saw the body did better than those who did not; and bereaved parents did worse than the other relatives. On general health scores, bereaved mothers did more poorly than any other group. On the judgments made from clinical interviews, mothers had the worst outcome, followed closely by fathers. In the total group considered to have reached a bad outcome, bereaved parents accounted for 70 percent.

In a study of normal bereavement, parents' symptoms compared to spouses' showed higher incidence of weight loss, instability, difficulty in concentrating, loss of interest in television, newspapers, and friends, depressed mood, crying, self-condemnation, and the use of medicines. They reported slightly lower symptoms of loss of interest in job or church. Remaining symptoms, such as sleep disturbances, suicidal thoughts, somatic symptoms, and tiredness, were reported at very close levels.[9]

Sanders, too, noted the difficult bereavements experienced by parents. Comparing adults who lost a parent, child, or spouse within the prior three months, she found that, in general, response to bereavement is more a function of the premorbid level of adjustment rather than the type of bereavement or the conditions under which it occurred. But, she goes on to note, the death of a child caused significantly greater bereavement reactions than did either the death of a spouse or parent.[10]

The conclusions from these studies and the preceding pages press us to look at those clinicians who have worked with cases of pathological mourning. These are the instances where people are already grieving abnormally, that is, they are locked somewhere in the process. Pathological grief can be manifested in any of the various forms discussed in Chapter Two. Some types of treatment, the rationale behind them, and the dynamics are described below.

One method of intervention was tried by Hodgkinson with hospitalized patients. He saw them two-to-three times a week in an attempt to attack denial of the loss. Patients selected were those who had severe but clear-cut grief problems. The assessment concentrated on highlighting the area of emotional pain or avoidance. The initial phase then concentrated on stimulating emotions, thereby acknowledging again and again that the death was real. To release inhibited emotions, the individuals were instructed to bring in an object that had a special connection with the deceased. The standard one was a photograph. Later, more specific objects were sometimes used, drawing on those that were either treasured or ignored. These are examples of what Volkan called "linking objects."[11] They are things that have powerful connections to the deceased and, in the extreme, come to be regarded as extensions of the dead individual, indicating difficulty in accepting reality. Confrontation with these objects creates an immediacy with the deceased, makes avoidance of reality difficult, and are intended to stimulate cathartic outbursts.

The second step in the treatment was the "third chair" exercise, a Gestalt technique of externalizing the conflict by talking with the deceased. The third stage was that of relinquishing the deceased, beginning to say goodbye. Hodgkinson does not differentiate by the type of loss suffered, although he mentions treating one bereaved father and one bereaved mother and notes improvement.[12]

Lieberman was another who researched problems of abnormal or morbid grief. He also conceptualized treatment as "forced mourning," comprised of three stages. First, the diagnosis was important in ascertaining whether or not the present symptoms were related to a past loss. If it was so decided, he explained the rationale of treatment to the patient and educated the individual to the normality of grieving and the essential nature of the process to well-being.

The second stage was a time of exploration, and treatment was centered on avoided emotions, using objects that previously had been ignored. The therapists' ability to tolerate strong emotional display reassured the patient of his or her own ability to handle intense emotions.

The third stage was reached when the patient was able to review the total relationship, acknowledging its positive and negative aspects; to put aside avoidance behavior; and to begin new relationships. The active participation of the therapist continued until the mourning was begun and included warm, empathic confrontation and legitimization of feeling. Lieberman noted importantly that other, old losses may be brought up in the term of treatment, and termination was again faced when the therapist/patient relationship was ended. Failure to address this latest termination could block the successful conclusion of therapy.

Lieberman found three distinct groups of people stuck in the mourning process. First, there were those who avoided grief by staying away from persons, things, and places connected with the deceased. Accompanying this behavior or mode of coping is usually anger and/or guilt about the deceased or the circumstances of the death. Often there was displacement, where the affect connects with external objects, which makes it similar to phobias and responsive to the forced mourning techniques.

The second group of people showed a lack of grieving or guilt, but a great deal of anger. Idealization of the dead occurs with the anger and resentment is frequently directed at doctors. These individuals tend to couple denial with projections of hostility outward. It can be expected the anger will, at some point in the treatment, be directed at the therapist before it can be redirected to the dead person.

The third group exhibited prolonged grief with physical symptoms; noted here were hypertensive cardiovascular disease, diabetes, duodenal ulcer, or asthma. The grief and physical symptoms were usually accompanied by nightmares. The dynamics here included displacement and introjection, resulting in symptoms and depression. The dynamics suggest treatment including a combination of interpretative techniques, stressing the dreams, coupled with behavioral interventions.

Lieberman is one of the few to point out that forced mourning can have negative consequences, heightening symptoms without the benefit of catharsis or insight.[13]

These are very different studies, focusing on different aspects of bereavement with different groups of people. Yet there are some striking similarities that join them. Integrating these findings with the knowledge gained from the bereaved mothers in this study, some ideas about maternal bereavement and intervention can be generated. First, bereaved parents constitute, in general, a high-risk group. Second, the norm for parental bereavement appears to be a very lengthy, intense mourning process, and application of previous standards of symptomatology may be ignoring this evidence. Third, it appears that even in the wide range of bereavement reactions, the dynamics of the process can be facilitated by knowledgeable and empathic responses, professional or otherwise. Fourth, for individuals such as bereaved parents who are likely to be at greater risk, intervention can be preventive. High risk can be reduced to low risk. The intervention here appears to encourage a normal mourning process. Fifth, for those people who are already blocked in the process, interventions can help to release the emotional response and allow it to proceed more normally, but there are risks and a well-structured setting is essential. Sixth, the concentration on focused short-term intervention is not to complete the mourning but to guide it so that the individual can complete it outside of treatment. But it remains questionable whether focusing short-term on salient themes for bereaved mothers will be useful because the death of a child calls up so many issues that are of a continuing and far-reaching nature.

USE OF COMPASSIONATE FRIENDS

> Until you walk in my shoes, God forbid . . . to know the pain that I've known is so, so terrible . . . . It's the end of everything, the end of dreams, the end of your future.
>
> (Anne)

Another important resource to be looked at is the use of self-help groups in coping with bereavement. The self-help group is one type of emotional and social support. The research addressing the use of others in reducing anxiety states dates back to the 1950s, and emotional supports have consistently been found to mitigate the effects of stress. But in a study of widows and widowers, supportive individuals were found to be useful in inhibiting the emotional display as well as facilitating the work of mourning.[14] It appears that any group with which the mourner can identify and receive what she perceives of as support, provides important resources in coping with bereavement.

The self-help group, as a support, then, has a unique place. Lieberman and Borman note:

> Traditionally, they have been defined as being composed of members who share a common condition, situation, heritage, symptom or experience. They emphasize self-reliance and generally offer a face-to-face or phone-to-phone fellowship network, available and accessible without charge. (p. 2)[15]

Yet they have some important similarities to professional systems being composed of people who are initially strangers, having a structure, experienced and informed participants, and requiring a commitment of energy and effort. It is a blend of some of the expectations of one's family and friends with aspects of more formalized professional service systems.

Extensive work has been done by Lieberman, Borman, and associates on self-help groups for coping with crises.[16] Several of the studies they report are based on data from Lieberman's Transitions Study, which was an attempt to link the nature of particular life crises or conditions with the responses in seeking external resources. The Transitions Study, begun in Chicago in 1972, was designed to analyze both the major events and changes in the lives of adults that require coping efforts, and the personal factors that are associated with effective resource utilization. Their studies were guided by four general hypotheses about why people seek out self-help groups. The first was that self-help groups arise to fulfill services not otherwise being met by other systems. Second, the alternative hypothesis was a "disappointment hypothesis" based on the observation that people use multiple resources and find self-help groups when they have not found the help elsewhere. Warheit had argued this hypothesis, positing that when a stressful event occurs, the first line of defense is the psychological, physical, and genetic make-up of the individual. If that is not sufficient, resources are sought from spouse, children, parents, and family. It proceeds to interpersonal networks of friends, professional persons, or agencies, and finally to culturally provided beliefs, values, and symbols. He acknowledged that in practice some or all are used simultaneously and in complementary fashion. It is likely that the use of these resources depends on whether or not support is actually perceived as forthcoming from that direction, and the nature and meaning of the loss.[17]

Lieberman's third hypothesis questioned whether individuals go to self-help groups because of the exchange of giving and receiving help and having to expand the least effort in locating this resource. Fourth, it is believed that these groups provide specialized services, the best fit between individual needs and services actually provided. These views are not mutually exclusive nor contradictory, and served to organize the investigations of the Transitions Study.

The self-help groups themselves differ in their aims. Some groups effect change in their members through behavioral control, and have been widely used in the treatment of alcoholism, obesity, and smoking. Others are stress-coping self-help groups, one of which is Compassionate Friends. This organization's aim is to enable members to adapt to life changes and, as such, it focuses more on adaptation and coping through internal, behavioral, attitudinal, or affective changes.

Compassionate Friends was also one of five self-help systems studied by Lieberman with regard to why people joined. Questionnaire items for this group differed somewhat from those given to the other groups, but all broadly examined the same goals: (1) social-hedonistic, those goals of meeting people and having fun; (2) endstate, the type of change desired, usually mental health goals; and (3) process goals, the experiences an individual would like to have as a result of joining. The variety of events and processes that appeared to be sought in the third category were divided into six subcategories: similarity-communion goals of sharing; cognitive-informative processes of learning; modeling from others who had similar experiences; emotional support; abreactive-cathartic dimensions of expressing emotions; and linkages with others.

In the responses received from members of Compassionate Friends, six out of the top seven reasons for joining were process goals:

> Individuals had an image of what kinds of events or experiences they desired in order to obtain some mastery over and relief from the devastating impact of losing a child. They wished to share their experiences with others who had been through the same event; they wanted to learn from others how to cope; they wanted to make contact with other bereaved parents who could become resources outside of the group setting; and they wanted to express their profound grief without fear of negative sanctions. (p. 47)[18]

There is a clear desire, despite the severity of the event, to attempt to control what would be most helpful to them. There is also a high correlation between the groups' stated goals and those of the individuals, so that a fit of individual and culture becomes apparent. The ideology, or belief system, of Compassionate Friends seems to match the needs of many bereaved parents.

Sherman described the emergence of ideology in this group. He chose three major predicaments: maladaptive responses, family relationships, and social reintegration, and explored how those situations were addressed by the ideology of Compassionate Friends.

Personal maladaptive responses

Denial, anger and guilt, and despair and depression were selected as significant maladaptive responses. The group response is to provide a place where the child is remembered and discussed, counteracting the desire to deny that the death occurred. The opening of the meeting insures this because the general format is one in which each person introduces himself or herself in turn and tells something about the child and how she/he died. Cognitive reconceptualization is also used to counter denial, anger and guilt, and despair. Presentations, literature, workshops, and sharing information encourage intellectual understanding, lessening of intense negative affect through the belief that it is all expectable in "normal" grieving, and gives parents a sense of personal mastery. The focus, in dealing with anger and guilt in particular, encourages forgiveness that approaches nonresponsibility. To mitigate the paralysis resulting from despair and depression, the group provides a safe place to remember and grieve, but simultaneously encourages a reinvestment in activities.

Problems in family relationships

There is great emphasis on keeping the marriage and family together. Both partners are encouraged to attend meetings and activities are often planned to include remaining children. The group offers suggestions for resolving marital conflicts and stresses the belief that it is the external stress of losing a child that causes the difficulties, not something within the relationship. They also teach that spouses and children have individual grieving styles and each must learn to tolerate the other's differences. Parents are encouraged to reinvest in remaining children but to avoid overprotection on one extreme or neglect through preoccupation on the other extreme.

Social reintegration

Members of the group are encouraged to be active in relationships; to teach friends that they need to talk about the child; to be tolerant of unintended mistakes of others; and to reach out to others. The ideological teaching is intended to offset intense feelings of isolation and alienation, allowing parents to function in the larger world.[19]

From these studies, Compassionate Friends emerges as a social system designed to provide its members with a variety of coping strategies enabling them to adjust to the death of a child. The strategies include providing literature, enabling discussions, and sharing practical information; offering new ways of cognitively conceptualizing their loss; and sharing experiences with similarly afflicted others. The sharing involves both giving and receiving, depending on the emotional needs of the parent. Compassionate Friends appears to provide, for its participants, a forum where bereaved parents can assume some mastery after an event that threatened to shatter their internal and external worlds.

Of the women interviewed, seven belonged to Compassionate Friends and nine did not. The two groups were of similar age, education, income, and in relationships with children, but there were several differences. The self-help group had all three of the women who had expressed guilt after the child's death, both women whose sons had been murdered, and more of the women who reported conflict in their marriages. Another major difference was that eight out of the nine nonmembers reported clergy as a resource during bereavement, whereas only two out of seven group members turned to clergy. The final distinction between the women in the two groups was that the self-help group members were often more at ease in describing their feelings and experiences, and more willing to do so. These interesting contrasts will be examined as the use and meaning of the self-help group is explored. (Tables 14, 15, and 16 in the Appendix compare members with nonmembers for all women studied.)

Compassionate Friends chapters usually meet once a month in the evenings and once during the daytime. Each meeting begins with those present introducing themselves and saying something about the child and how he or she died. Some meetings have specific topics for discussion, speakers, or programs. Other meetings are open to any topic raised by people attending.

Women said they attend meetings and value the Compassionate Friends organization because it provides the shared experience of being with others who have been through the same tragedy; it brings them into contact with people who will understand, whereas "others might come with nets"; it is a group which teaches that the woman is "normal" and all feelings are acceptable; it provides some answers to the problems that plague bereaved mothers; and, in the tradition of self-help groups, it is a place where women can give help as well as receive it.

The shared experience was mentioned by most of the women and highly valued. They needed to be with people who had undergone the same loss and they trusted the compassion and advice of these others.

They said that if another bereaved mother gave them advice or criticism, it was believed and accepted more readily. The related belief that *only other bereaved parents could understand* was expressed equally often. Jane said that words were meaningless because the depth of the pain could not be communicated. Therefore, only someone who had been through it could know. This not only refers to the event, but to the strange feelings and thoughts they experience.

These two themes help in explaining why, in both the interview and questionnaire sample, there were more group members among those women who had conflicted marriages. There were no differences in importance of spouse, but of those marital relationships that showed change during this period, more wives attended Compassionate Friends meetings. It appears that it is not the level of importance of the spouse, but the instability of the relationship that correlates with group use. This idea is also congruent with the higher percentage of separated and divorced women who are group members. Because the importance of the spouse is very significant during this time, disruption in this relationship or perceived lack of support appears likely to encourage the need for outside support and resources.

One problem that can arise from the belief that only other bereaved parents can understand is that the mother holds on to the pain by the belief in its uniqueness, and creates additional isolation from others. Marion noted that a "danger" of Compassionate Friends was the tendency to create a we/they split, believing that *only* other bereaved parents could understand, drawing them closer, but seeing the world as an unsympathetic enemy. It appears that in the extreme, the self-help group fulfills the function of allowing the mothers to hold on to the child and to continue grieving but may not facilitate the more lengthy adaptation of letting go, even of the pain. Thelma, in trying to describe her experience of the self-help group and why she stopped going after 1½-2 years, discussed her discomfort. She said that she would be sad when she returned home and felt that she had reached the point where she no longer wanted to feel that way. She asked, "What is it to work out your grief?" It appears that the usefulness of the constant remembering and discussion was gone. She wondered, after four years, if she had grieved enough, and worked it through. She seemed ready to move in the direction noted previously, to relinquish pain.

The third theme, that of *being "normal"* and not alone, gave the women the permission they needed to grieve in their own way without the anxiety of feeling "crazy." By comparing notes with others, and listening to other reactions to a child's death, their own responses become more acceptable to them. They had not previously dealt with emotions of such intensity and were relieved to see that others experienced the same thing and had coped with it. Continuing to go to meetings provided a place to grieve after other resources had run dry. The self-help group became a secure place, sometimes needed most when friends and family had gotten tired of the bereavement and pushed the woman to return to normal. For some, it was the only place that was exclusively for remembering the child and discussing ongoing problems of theirs, their marriage, or their relationships with family and friends.

The theme of being "normal" is useful in understanding why the mothers of homicide victims tended to be members. The women noted that the rarity of losing a child is already an "abnormal" experience. Murder, as a cause, is particularly unique. The self-help group provides a place where they can find similar, if not exact, types of loss, normalizing the experience as well as the reactions to it. Self-help groups have recently been started specifically for the parents of children who have been murdered, supporting the idea that people look for a shared experience and others who will understand that loss.

It was also noted, from questionnaire data, that women who have lost more than one child tend to be group users. The same dynamic applies in these cases. The group provides some guides about feelings and answers to questions, and it is a place for these mothers who have been struck by the tragedy more than once to be with other people who have had terrible times. One of the things mentioned in interviews was the feeling that there are people "worse off" at the meetings, and that is a source of comfort. The search for "similar others" is very important in understanding the group experience. Where else can they find people who can understand a double or triple loss?

The fourth theme, *getting answers,* was an interesting one that dealt with the day-to-day problems that are common to this group and no other. For example, how do you answer the question, "How many children do you have?" The group also sponsors speakers, discussions, programs for siblings, and reading material on how to cope with the death of a child. The stress is always on normalcy; every feeling that a parent experiences is okay and due to the stress of the death. The attitude toward marital discord is the same; it results from the event of losing the child. The groups encourage people to "do their own thing" about holidays, rituals, and idiosyncratic behaviors. By these discussions, they also help anticipate future problems, such as difficulties with remaining children, how to talk to friends about the loss, and the duration of the process of mourning. Getting answers means more than what to do or say. It is a way of reconceptualizing grief reactions as normal, a reassuring thought to people who are intensely grieving.

The final theme the women articulated was that the group provided *an opportunity to help others* with their grief. In the beginning, they saw themselves as receiving help, but for those women who stayed in the group there was a shift to giving help to newly bereaved parents. They like to be able to help others, to have their time occupied in ways they considered constructive, and to direct the emotions connected to the loss into channels that were creative. Patty said that her work with other parents "can't take the pain away, but I can sure help them to know the kind of road and that's helpful." Some people stop attending the group when they have been helped; others remain and become helpers. For many of these women, helping others provides a great deal of satisfaction for them. Sandy, who does not attend meetings but is involved in church-related activities, said,

> You help yourself when you tell someone "it's okay the way you're dealing with it." At the same time you're telling yourself the same thing.

The self-help group keeps some members for a long time. They become the helpers as their own mourning process subsides. Others may be coming to grips with the loss after a long period of time elapsed without resolution. Marion noted that, after years, the self-help group is the place set aside "once a month" to remember the child.

The final theme, helping others, is altruistic. It parallels the previous discussion of the satisfactions of motherhood. It was stated then that women gain in satisfaction and development from the child's growth. The mothers here are also receiving satisfaction from helping others. It can also further the resolution of the loss and gratify the desire to nurture.

The women who did not attend meetings of Compassionate Friends said that they did not go because they "never got around to it," or, in two instances, they had gone once but did not like the bitterness or the depression they saw there. Their attitudes were marked by determination to accept the death and to make the best of their situation.

Often women who did not attend meetings said they looked forward to the newsletters and mentioned the themes previously discussed. They saw the newsletters as giving them advice and reassurance.

It appears that women must be ready to talk about the experience publicly or they would not seek a self-help group. The group facilitates their understanding of the experience and reassures them so that they can continue to talk about it and try to understand. The group encourages already existing curiosity and questioning natures. Those who are more private, inhibited, involved in less formal support groups or do not want this experience avoid it.

The other significant dynamic that emerged from this data is that even nonmembers of the group get help and support in another way. Many of the nonmembers, as mentioned earlier, turned to the clergy and religion, and became participants in religious activities. Sherry, whose daughter had been killed with friends, had a neighborhood support group. It was informal; they did not always talk about the children or the deaths, but they met almost daily. Sylvia, who worked at the hospital where her daughter was brought, was surrounded by friends who knew as much as she did about the death. Their support continued. These women had friends who listened, family, religion, books, workshops on grief and bereavement, and work. The results of examining support systems indicate that women received a great deal of help and comfort from a variety of sources.

These professional, self-help, organized religious and informal social groups provide some essential forms of help. Groups have always perpetuated our cultural system and given meaning to losses. There we see that groups not only establish norms but also help to reestablish individual equilibrium and connectedness with others that had been ruptured. Through the support provided, women are helped to learn how to rejoin society.

Pollock discussed the social psychological understanding of group mourning and the ways it aids adaptation. Commonly ascribed-to rituals provide the individual or group with a means of reintegrating with the community, but stringent rituals are more often found in primitive societies than sophisticated ones, such as ours. In all groups, the sharing of thoughts, feelings, and activities assists cohesiveness with each other in spite of the loss of one valued member. The communication of common grief and pain solidifies the group, permits hope, and allows continuity to gradually take over, often paralleling the individual internal mourning process.[20]

Mourning has been presented as an intense emotional process, during which time the mother must adapt to a changed reality. We now see some of the social implications for the woman and her relationships with others.

As seen, emotional supports are essential during the first year. The women have many resources available and value them. They appear to seek help from different people depending on their needs. Of utmost importance are the desires to be heard and understood, to be comforted by intimate relationships, and to have dependency needs met without sacrificing attempts at mastery.

NOTES

1. Nancy Gourash, "Help-seeking: A Review of the Literature," *American Journal of Psychology, 6,* no.5 (1978): 413-423.

2. Gerald Gurin, Joseph Veroff and Sheila Feld, *Americans View Their Mental Health: A Nationwide Survey* (New York: Basic Books, 1960).

3. Marjorie Fisk Lowenthal and Clayton Haven, "Interaction and Adaptation: Intimacy, a Critical Variable," *American Sociological Review, 33,* Part 1 (1968): 20-30.

4. Gerald Gurin et al., *Americans View Their Mental Health.*

5. William Alexy, "Dimensions of Psychological Counseling That Facilitate the Grieving Process of Bereaved Parents," *Journal of Counseling Psychology, 29,* no.5 (1982): 498-507.

6. Beverley Raphael, "Preventive Intervention with Recently Bereaved," *Archives of General Psychiatry, 34* (Dec. 1977): 1450-1454.

7. Colin Murray Parkes, "Bereavement Counseling: Does It Work?" *British Medical Journal, 5* (July, 1980): 3-6.

8. Bruce Singh and Beverley Raphael, "Postdisaster Morbidity of the Bereaved: A Possible Role for Preventive Psychiatry?" *The Journal of Nervous and Mental Disease, 169,* no.4 (April, 1981): 203-212.

9. Paula Clayton, Lynn Desmarais, and George Winokur, "A Study of Normal Bereavement," *American Journal of Psychiatry, 125* (1968): 168-178.

10. Catherine Sanders, "A Comparison of Adult Bereavement in the Death of a Spouse, Child and Parent," *Omega, 10,* no.4 (1979-1980): 303-321.

11. Vamik Volkan, A.F. Ciluffo, and T.L. Sarvay, "Re-grief Therapy and the Function of the Linking Object as a Key to Stimulate Emotionality" in *Emotional Flooding,* ed. P. Olsen (New York: Human Sciences Press, 1976).

12. Peter E. Hodgkinson, "Abnormal Grief—The Problem of Therapy," *British Journal of Medical Psychology, 55* (1982): 29-34.

13. Stuart Lieberman, "Nineteen Cases of Morbid Grief," *British Journal of Psychiatry, 132* (1978): 159-163.

14. Ira Glick et al., *The First Year.*

15. Morton Lieberman, Lawrence Borman and Associates, *Self-Help Groups for Coping with Crisis.*

16. Ibid.

17. George Warheit, "Life Events, Coping, Stress and Depressive Symptomatology," *American Journal of Psychiatry, 136* (1979): 413-507.

18. Morton Lieberman, Lawrence Borman, and Associates, *Self-Help Groups.*

19. Barry Sherman, "The Emergence of Ideology in a Bereaved Parents Group" in *Self-help Groups for Coping with Crisis.* Morton Lieberman, Lawrence Borman, and Associates (San Francisco: Jossey-Bass, 1979).

20. George Pollock, "On Mourning and Anniversaries: The Relationship of Culturally Constituted Defensive Systems to Intrapsychic Adaptive Processes," *Israel Annals of Psychiatry, 10,* no.1 (1972): 9-40.

nine

Rethinking the Problem

This work is not the first to suggest that parental bereavement is likely to precipitate a more difficult mourning process than many other types of deaths. Both Freud and Gorer wrote, without further explanation, that they supposed it to be so.[1] The few comparative studies available, Singh and Raphael, Clayton, and Sanders, note the same thing.[2] This book does attempt, however, to try to understand why maternal bereavement is so devastating, and how women adapt to this particular loss. It therefore becomes useful in the last chapter to see where the questioning has led us, and to bring together some of the ideas that have been developed throughout the book.

In any bereavement, it is necessary to understand who is lost—a child, spouse, parent, friend, hero; the meaning of that person; the aspects of the relationship; the personality and history of both the deceased and the mourner; the context and circumstances of the loss; the preparation or suddenness of the death; the survivor's available resources; and societal and cultural meaning of the loss. These different variables are important. Attention to them makes the uniqueness of each experience more understandable. But if some generalization is not possible if each instance must be treated as being totally distinct from all others, then we are unable to learn from one experience to the next.

Figure 9-1 presents an overview of the process of maternal bereavement, identifying these significant variables. The influences are both

FIGURE 9-1. Overview of the Process of Maternal Bereavement.

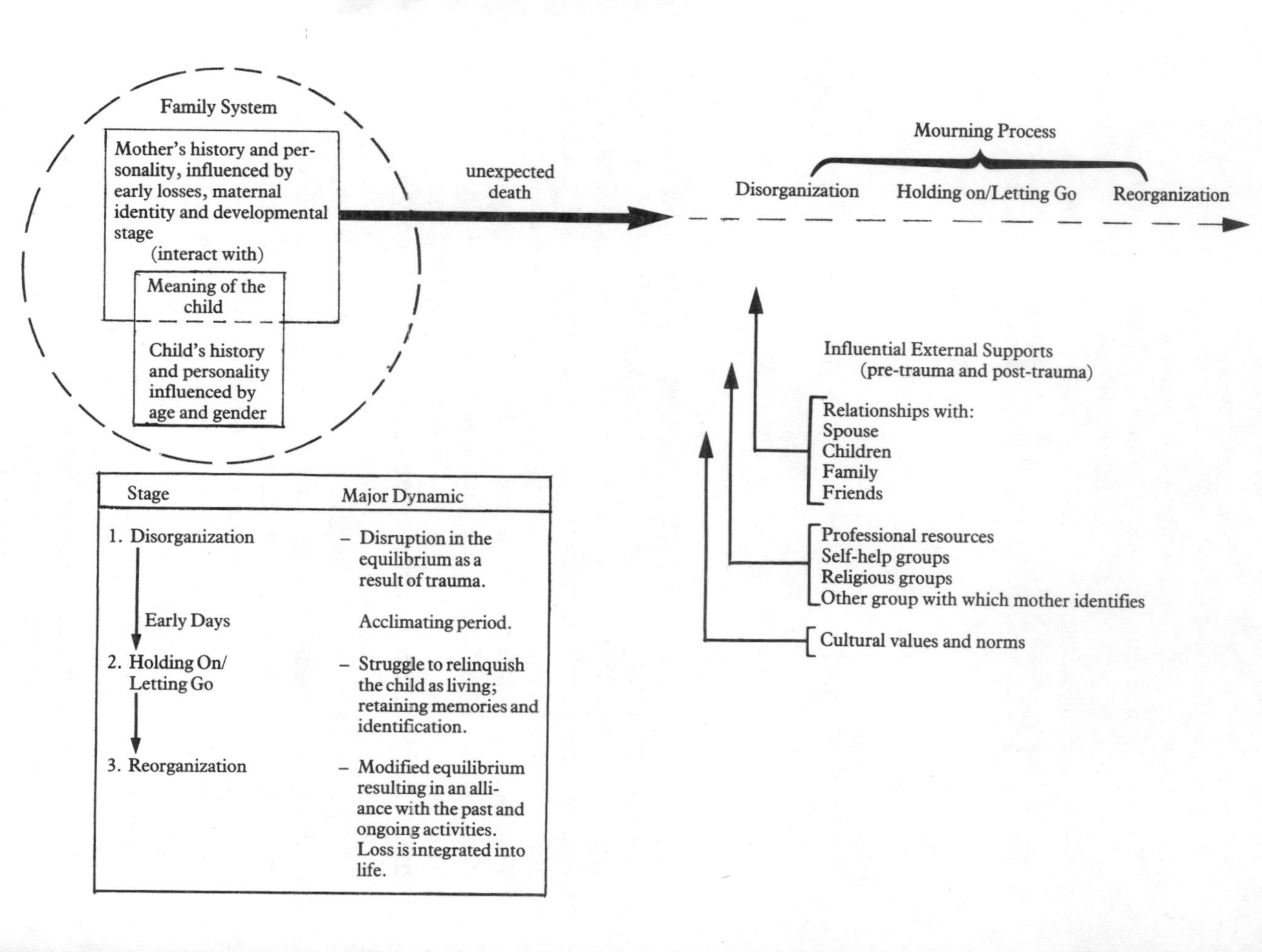

Stage	Major Dynamic
1. Disorganization	– Disruption in the equilibrium as a result of trauma.
Early Days	Acclimating period.
2. Holding On/ Letting Go	– Struggle to relinquish the child as living; retaining memories and identification.
3. Reorganization	– Modified equilibrium resulting in an alliance with the past and ongoing activities. Loss is integrated into life.

internal and external. The woman, and all she brings to mothering, interacts with the child's unique characteristics and personal meaning. This is a special dyad that exists interdependently within the family system. The unexpected death precipitates the process of mourning. First, the stage of disorganization involves an involuntary contraction of ego processes. The disorganization is adaptive to trauma. Although it means initially turning away from reality, rejecting change, it protects the mother from excessive stimulation caused by the magnitude of the event. Existing research has concentrated on the passivity and numbness of this period, neglecting the importance of realistic decision making. Such activity fulfills certain important functions for the mother. It binds in affect by keeping her busy. Otherwise she would be preoccupied, if not overwhelmed, by thoughts of the death. Decision making also provides the opportunity to move from a passive to an active position, assuming some mastery in a helpless situation. In these early days, we already see the beginnings of the struggle against overwhelming helplessness.

The second stage, that of holding on/letting go, is grounded in the specialness of the mother/child relationship. She suffers from despair at the loss of control of her life and her world. She is acutely sensitive to stimuli, often with a depth of feeling never before experienced. This is a lengthy adjustment to a changed reality. She has to painfully learn what aspects of the child can be kept and what must be relinquished in the service of her own growth and adaptation.

In the third stage of mourning, reorganization, developmental changes become more apparent. Although coping began immediately, the nature of the compromises shifts during the process. This final stage is marked by renewed activities and an integration of the loss into an ongoing life structure. This modified equilibrium allows an alliance with the past and a life in the present.

Bereavement is an internal activity but influenced strongly by certain external supports, existing both before and after the event. Of particular importance are intimate relationships wtih a partner, remaining children if any, family, and friends. There are also professional resources such as doctors, clergy, and therapists who provide different kinds of help. More informal supports include self-help groups, workshops, religious groups, educational experiences, work activities, and any other group with which the woman can identify. Finally, the cultural and societal values cannot be ignored. These vague but powerful influences give meaning to people and events, dictate behaviors, and reward and censure thoughts and acts.

These parameters help to distinguish the death of a child from other deaths and to summarize the process. But this raises the question, "What does the mother lose with the death of a child?" This study has described three interrelated types of loss that occur when a child dies: (1) the loss of an aspect of the mother herself; (2) the loss of future hopes and expectations; and (3) the loss of illusions.

The death of a child assaults maternal identity. The death as a loss of self is partly understood as related to the shared physical attachment during pregnancy, a symbiotic attachment in the child's infancy, and the ever-present adjustments and absorption during the years of mothering. The care and the investment have been great, with the roots of maternal emotions and behaviors in the mother's own childhood. The death is likely to injure her self-esteem. She must grapple with the feeling that she has somehow failed. To full acknowledge the total lack of existence of the child is to relinquish a part of who the mother is.

The loss of future hopes and expectations was of an intensely personal nature. Children are usually thought of as an aspect of the parents' immortality but, in a strange reversal, the mother now has the responsibility of insuring that the child lives on in memories or memorials. The mothers mourned all that the child could have become; they also mourned for themselves. They, too, were stopped "midstream" and denied their own expectations for the future.

The third loss, that of illusions, was another contributing factor to the affect of the mourning process. The beliefs in security and protection, fairness and control, and answers and questions were destroyed for some women. The death of a child is an uncomparably "wrong" event. There is little that feels so innately unjust and against the order of nature as the death of a child. The mother is pitched into a dangerous world. Society contributes by prizing children, and through advances in science, by increasing our unfamiliarity with early deaths.

It is this very special relationship, that of a mother and her child, that can cause these kinds of deeply scarring and far-reaching losses.

The mourning process for bereaved mothers is lengthy and painful, more so than other bereavement studies have documented. From the disorganization of first hearing the news, through the struggle of holding on/letting go, to eventual reorganization, the process will take years. The dynamics of maternal bereavement have been described in the past pages. The woman is faced with a helplessness that is uniquely powerful. Her identity is disturbed. Much of her work is allowing this loss to become a part of who she is now but without making it her complete existence. It is not all she is, but it will be, for an endless time, an important aspect of who she is and who she will become.

The stress, of course, is not confined to the mother alone. The ramifications of her bereavement and the grief of her family permeate the home. Deborah's son reacted strongly to his younger sister's death from a car accident. His behavior worsened and steadily upset his parents more and more:

> And at one time when things were the worst with him, and I was angry and bitter, I said, "My God, that man didn't just murder our daughter, he murdered our whole family."

The isolation that can come with deep grief may separate the husband and wife. He, too, is dealing with the death of his child. The wife may blame herself or her husband; perhaps, he does the same. Surely, with the absorption of mourning, there is an impaired ability to respond to one's partner. The remaining children, often reminders of the loss, are suffering the loss of a sibling and the distraction of parents. Depending on their level of development, children mourn differently from their parents. Very young children respond more to the change in parents than to any reality of death. Awareness of the permanence is a later understanding. Even adolescents have a different cognition of the experience than do adults; children have a great deal to handle. They may be burdened by unspeakable guilt over past fights or destructive wishes; friends may be insensitive; feelings that they don't understand threaten to overwhelm them. They, too, are survivors, and pay a price. They may rework the sibling's death again and again as they mature. The affects are certainly long lasting and far reaching.

For the family, the world has changed. If people treat them too differently it is uncomfortable. If people treat them as they were in the past, it is insulting. The death can bring many additional problems. Job dissatisfaction may become severe, fear of making mistakes or the inability to concentrate may interfere with previously satisfying work, or priorities may be reevaluated. Other problems may result indirectly from the death. Financial problems occur because of medical treatments for the child, or maybe for stress-related illnesses that develop later in another family member. All members of the family have decisions to make. Women question whether they want to remain in the same community or move away from the memories—what do they do about holidays? What do they tell strangers? How should they behave in public and private? What can they expect in the future? They wonder when mourning will end, if they ever will feel a joy of living, and what they will be like when the worst of it is finally over. For some women, the most painful thought of all is a fear that they will forget the child. There are equally strong, conflicting desires—to feel whole again and be free of pain, but to keep as much as possible of the child alive.

> I am thinking . . . maybe when he was killed last week or so, sure, that is okay to mention. But as it gets to be longer and longer I wonder, do people still expect you to mention that you had him and he was killed? Someday it's going to be 20 years.
>
> (Louise)

All this combines to create a mourning process that goes on indefinitely. The women said, "You don't get over it." The rupture in their lives cannot be undone. Successful mourning is the adaptation to this profound change. The nature of coping shifts throughout the bereavement and the changes were seen as being not bound by time, but did tend to predominate at different periods. The first year found the women preoccupied with the loss. Thoughts of the dead child were ever-present, although by the end of that year life activities were under way again and serious symptoms had subsided. The women remained acutely sensitive to the loss, reminders were frequent, and painful affective reactions continued.

It seems that at the end of the first year, much of the outward life is back to the way that it was or is changed but stabilized; the somatic complaints diminish, relationships return to more normalcy, but the mourning continues on and on. It was less visible—the devotion became more internal than behavioral. The attachment between mother and child is powerful and it is a mistake to conceptualize maternal mourning as ending in a year. Also, the guidelines that are often used for understanding pathological mourning are not always useful for bereaved mothers. It is not unusual for mothers, in that first year, to hear voices, have conversations with the dead child, feel that she could go crazy, want to die, and experience intense prolonged depression and helplessness. For the woman to know this, and for the helping professionals to understand it, allows her to experience the full range of her emotions without feeling abnormal or additionally out of control.

Although existing work outlines the sequential stages of mourning, it has a recurring nature. There is much oscillation as the struggles are not fought and won, but faced again and again. Progress is seen as the difficulties become less frequent, less intense, of shorter duration, easier to understand, and balanced by healthy gratifying activity.

An example of the repetitive conflicts was seen in two clear instances when parents came across unexpected pictures of the child one year later. They reported the shock symptoms just like those felt when they first heard the news of the death, but these passed more quickly. Understanding that there are intense progressive and regressive elements to the process helps reduce anxiety and increases tolerance in both parents and professionals. Most studies of bereavement end here at this first year. The clarity of this period diminishes, but the process is not ended.

At approximately the end of the second year, the mothers appeared to be searching for new directions and trying to find meaning in the loss. The women wanted to help others and themselves, mostly in nurturing ways and connected with the loss. For some, there was a shift in self-help group participation from being helped to becoming the helper. Others found career possibilities that were related to restitutive efforts, such as working with children. Still others kept the child's death separated from the remainder of their activities. The women were beginning to deal with questions of guilt over experiencing pleasure because it meant forgetting the child. This year also brought a greater realization of the enduring nature of the loss. Acceptance of the death was beginning to mean irrevocable change.

The third year brought greater levels of acceptance, and individualized coping styles were strongly in evidence. Those women who tended to be accepting and unquestioning were entrenched in that position. Those who continued to pursue the meaning of the experience were able to find constructive ways of doing so. They had begun to integrate the loss into the fabric of their lives and personalities. They pursued different paths. Some were involved in altruistic activities somewhat related to the death but that were also compatible with the mother's personality.

> She will always be a vivid part of this family, never forgotten. Maybe not a growing, living, breathing part, but a very important part. Just coming to grips with the fact that I was never going to get over it, that I would live with it, was a big help . . . I had the feeling in the beginning that I'm gonna get over this and is it going to be good when it finally passes. All these years go by and I'm not over it and it doesn't

> feel good. You have to go in a different direction then . . . I've incorporated it into my life.
>
> (Patty, six years later)

In this group of women who lost a child more than three years before, we see an opportunity that grief presented to one individual. The possibility always exists that the resolution of present loss can repair injuries of the past.

Thelma was one of five women in this study who suffered a major loss in childhood. Her mother had died when she was seven years old. Thelma was open and questioning, willing to explore the meaning and experience of her son's death. Some of the reasons became clear during the meeting. She said that she had been manic-depressive for years, on medication that managed the problem, and intermittently in therapy. In discussing her depression, she said that it had lifted after the death of her son, and episodes of depression had become shorter since that time. She began to wonder if it had something to do with the loss of her mother and questioned the grief that she "had carried for years" as a result of that death. It appears that her son's death had enabled her to reopen the earlier experience, and in her mourning for the son, she also mourned the death of her mother. The result has been a lessening of the depressive condition. It took a loss of the magnitude of her son's death to reach the grief that lingered from the loss of her mother, and successful mourning in the second instance brought some freedom from the burden of the prior death. This is only a single instance, but the implication is clear that later losses can, because of their power to evoke earlier ones, provide opportunities for resolution.

There were other women, too, who had suffered losses in early childhood. Some of them were difficult to interview because they appeared to have developed an acceptance towards life's tragedies that the rest of the mothers did not possess. They were agreeable to answering questions but there was a resistance to inquiry that could shake carefully laid foundations. There was no doubt that these women experienced grief at the loss of their children and mourned them, but the ways that they had evolved in dealing with life, plus the amount of time that had passed, put up barriers to exploration. Over and over, they explained in different ways that they learned long ago "life is unfair" or "you just have to go on," "there is nothing I can do, I have to accept it." Prior losses appear to play a very significant part in adaptation to present loss, in both hindering and facilitating the woman's ability to examine and cope.

This kind of finding raises questions for clinical work and research. Even knowing the significant variables, prediction is still beyond us. Other researchers have occasionally noted that some people who, by all available assessments, should not do well, go on to fine adjustments. The reverse is also true. Some individuals with apparent internal strengths and outside support get blocked in healthy adaptation. Longitudinal studies would be very useful in following people over time and would teach us more about the long-term outcomes of bereavement—how loss is continually integrated into the fabric of individual lives. Another need is development of prospective studies, early assessment of individuals as they normally develop, confronting a variety of life stresses.

We have seen that the dynamics of the process may be universal but there are elements that are special to loss of a child and, further, that individual reactions vary greatly. People respond differently when confronted by the same problem. Louise spoke poignantly about the helplessness, Thelma about the guilt, Ellen about the terror when problems developed with her remaining children, Sylvia about the loneliness, Anne about the suicidal despair, and Jane about the unfairness of her world. These themes were not all that any of them experienced, and they were not the only ones to talk about the issue, but the uniqueness and individuality of each experience was there.

Significantly, even when their perceptions were different, their needs were surprisingly similar. When they talked about some of the problems that they faced, and the people who provided help, five patterns of assistance were identified: shared experience and mutuality; availability and not withdrawing; having been through the same experience; forcing the mourner to go on living; and having performed specific tasks. In the light of the analyses of the problems these women encountered after the death of the child, the value of these supportive acts become apparent, and both self-help group members and nonmembers reported these themes.

The self-help group, as the members describe it, was a useful organization for different reasons. The value of Compassionate Friends was seen primarily as sharing the experience with others who have experienced the same tragedy. Women believed group members would understand whereas others could not. From them she learns that she is "normal" and that all feelings are acceptable. The group also provides some answers to the problems that arise as a result of the death. Finally, it is a place where mothers can give help as well as receive it.

Most women do not go further than family, friends, and informal supports. But what about those women who seek professional help, and what about the therapists who will work with them? Doctors have talked about how painful it is to deal with parents of a dying child, to deliver the news, to be unable to "do anything." Nurses and social workers also have voiced their own pain at dealing with these families. It is not easy to be around death and grief. Doctors and nurses are aware that in spite of doing their best it may not save the child; they may be the recipients of the parents' harsh anger or lawsuits. Parents are not the only ones who feel the helplessness. To be empathic to the despair but not to become despairing can be difficult.

> An encounter with a grieving person is not very satisfying for anybody. You know, certainly not satisfying for the griever, and it's not satisfying for the helper, because neither one can give the other what they want. So you end up feeling a bit scrambled at times. I remember being so angry that somehow I couldn't get enough help, and then over a period of time realizing finally that, that I was getting enough help. Not at any one given time, but over, over a period of probably six or eight months, I began to have periods of feeling, feeling much better.
>
> (Lydia)

Therapeutic intervention has its own difficulties and gratifications. Models for dealing with pathological bereavement were discussed in the previous chapter. But what about this majority of bereaved parents—intensely grieving but not blocked in the process?

At a major psychological convention last year, a group of psychologists and graduate students met to talk about parental bereavement. An emotional discussion erupted when a woman asked, "What can I *do?*" as if help was always some act or behavior.

One significant form of help is empathy, that complex phenomenon of standing in the other's shoes, yet still keeping a foot in one's own—to be with, but to be able to distinguish betwen self and other. For the therapist, empathy is, in part, an identification with the mother. For the woman, it provides reassurance: that someone else has entered her world and respects her integrity; that her experiences can be understood; and that she is acceptable. Empathic communication teaches that she is not alone and that her thoughts and feelings, while intense, are tolerable and understandable to someone else, thereby making them more tolerable and understandable to her.

But what about the therapist, counselor, member of the clergy, doctor or nurse who has a professional relationship with a bereaved mother? The professional, in allowing herself or himself to truly experience the inner world of the mother, is confronted with significant issues. We have seen that the dynamics of maternal bereavement are not easily understandable or quickly resolvable. The helper, in sharing the experience, allows it to become a part of his or her world too. This may result in extreme reactions in the helper. Excessive responses could include rigidity or withdrawal, or, overinvolvement, leading to a loss of boundaries of one's self. Either extreme renders the helper ineffective.

The reactions occur because the professionals face the reactivation of their own fears, needs and unresolved personal issues about loss and death. The dynamics of loss and adaptation are easily ones with which to identify. In empathizing with the mother's loss, personal anxieties may be reawakened and old losses returned to consciousness. These dilemmas are integral in any therapeutic relationship, not only in working with bereaved parents, but it is important for the professional to remain aware of the areas of his or her own vulnerability in working with grieving adults.

Anyone who cannot conceptualize help as empathic response, sometimes listening, but feels the need to be active to "do" something, will have a difficult and unsuccessful time with these ideas about loss, mourning, and adaptation. Understanding is also help, as is tolerance, compassion and patience. Old losses will come back, old wounds reopened. The opportunities will be there. Old wounds can be understood and healed with the new ones, freeing the woman. In all treatment there is the opportunity to keep the mourning on the right track, to open and facilitate whatever degree of emotion or exploration is possible and desirable at the time, to help with family problems and understanding, to discuss the myriad emotions, to normalize the experience, encourage early mobilization of other empathic supports, provide reasonable expectations in coping, and encourage attempts at mastery.

Mourning is letting go of the past as it was, allowing a productive life in the present. Adjustment to a loss of this magnitude necessitates change. A new identity is forming—it may never be apparent to others, life may go on outwardly as before, but, for most, a profound transformation has taken place.

I want to give the last words of this book to the women. Lydia articulated the fear, the hope, the reality of going forward:

> Six or seven months after she died it suddenly occurred to me that this was no guarantee or insurance against further loss. That I could lose my son, that I could lose my husband, or that I could die, you know, what do you do with that? How do you deal with that? The temptation is to withdraw and to isolate myself, protect myself, not to take the risk of continuing to care in the face of that maybe happening again. Seems to me that it is one of the basic choices that as human beings we all have to make. Somehow I decided that I prefer to throw my hat in the ring and take my lumps, than try to protect myself from further loss because that has its own pain.

NOTES

1. Sigmund Freud in L. Binswanger, *Sigmund Freud: Reminiscences of a Friendship* (New York: Grune and Stratton, 1957); George Gorer, *Death, Grief and Mourning* (London: Cressent Press, 1965).

2. Bruce Singh and Beverley Raphael, "Preventive Intervention"; Paula Clayton et al., "A Study of Normal Bereavement"; Catherine Sanders, "A Comparison of Adult Bereavement"; George Pollock, "Temporal Anniversary Manifestations."

Appendix

Sample Questionnaire
SIDE 1

I am involved in a long-term research project about the experience of mourning for bereaved mothers who have lost children, and how that affects the other important relationships in her life, especially with her remaining children. Very little is known about these problems and I would greatly appreciate it if you would take the time to complete these questionnaires. If, in addition to this, you would be willing to be interviewed and/or complete a more extensive questionnaire, please fill out the bottom portion of this sheet. If an interview is not possible, I would still value the anonymous information contained in the upper portion. All information will remain confidential and will be used exclusively for the purpose of studying and helping bereaved mothers.

Thank you.

(Interviewer's Name
Institution—Phone)

Date ____________________

PLEASE ANSWER THE FOLLOWING QUESTIONS ABOUT YOURSELF:

Age __________ Race __________________ Primary occupation ______________________________

Religion ________________________ Highest grade of schooling completed ____________________

Marital Status ____________________ Approximate family income __________________________

Whom did you turn to for help after the death of your child? ________________________________

____

In what order? ____

Who were the most helpful? ____

Do you attend meetings of Compassionate Friends? Often _______ Occasionally _______ Never _______

PLEASE ANSWER THE FOLLOWING QUESTIONS ABOUT YOUR FAMILY:

Age of child at death ____________________ Gender of child ______________________________

Cause of death ____________________________________ Date of death ____________________

Present ages of remaining children ______________________ M or F ____________________ M or F

____________________ M or F

____

To what extent do you feel that grief still affects your daily life and activities?

____

____

****

This questionnaire is one portion of the study of mourning. If you would be willing to complete a more extensive questionnaire and/or be interviewed at your convenience for about 1-2 hours, please include your name, address and phone number. Thanks very much.

Questionnaire only ___________ Interview only ___________ Interview and Questionnaire ___________

Name ____ Phone number ________________

Address ____

Comments ____

____

SIDE 2

Please list, by first name or initials, the people in each of the categories below who were or are important to you during the experience of your child's death. If no people in a category are important to you, leave it blank.

(For each person you list, answer the questions in columns A through E)

	A	B	C					D					E				
	AGE	SEX M or F	HOW IMPORTANT WAS THIS PERSON TO YOU *BEFORE* YOUR CHILD'S DEATH?					HOW IMPORTANT WAS THIS PERSON IN THE *YEAR* FOLLOWING YOUR CHILD'S DEATH?					HOW IMPORTANT IS THIS PERSON TO YOU *NOW*?				
			VERY				NOT VERY	VERY				NOT VERY	VERY				NOT VERY
			1	2	3	4	5	1	2	3	4	5	1	2	3	4	5
1. SPOUSE/ PARTNER																	

2. FAMILY/ RELATIVE (instead of name, enter relation here—e.g., sister, mother, daughter, father, etc.)

3. CO-WORKERS (include friends who are co-workers here)

4. SUPERVISORS

5. PROFESSIONALS (instead of name, enter profession of person—e.g., doctor, clergy, psychiatrist)

6. FRIENDS (not already mentioned)

NOW, PLEASE GO BACK AND CIRCLE THE PERSON IN EACH GROUP WHO WAS OR IS *MOST* IMPORTANT TO YOU.
WHY? ____________________

This is an amended version of a questionnaire used by T. Antonucci, 1980, University of Michigan.

The *questionnaire* was a 25-item instrument designed to elicit information in the following areas:

A. A total of 16 background and sociodemographic items asked for age, marital status, occupation, religion, income; whom the women turned to after the child's death; in what order; who were the most helpful; whether they attended meetings of Compassionate Friends; age of the child at the time of death; cause of death; and ages of remaining children. The seventeenth item requested a statement as to the extent that grief affects the woman's daily life and activities.

B. Part One of the questionnaire ended with a request for an interview and/or further questionnaire.

C. Part Two of the questionnaire was a six-category scale assessing support networks. It asked for lists of people (spouse, family, coworkers, supervisors, professionals, and friends) and a ranking from 1-5 of their importance *before* the death of the child, in the *year following* the death, and *at present.* It further requested that the mother circle the person in each category who was most helpful, and why.

This questionnaire, as noted previously, was useful in sample selection, providing the information on women who do not fit the criteria for interviews and on women who chose to participate to this extent but refused to be interviewed.

The questionnaire data were analyzed in the following ways: Side 1, sociodemographic information was coded and examined through the use of frequency distributions and other descriptive techniques. Side 2 was analyzed by correlation and contingency tables, noting the changes in perceived support received from important individuals over time. Tables 5-13 and answers to open-ended questions were transcribed and examined for themes.

The rationale for the blend of quantitative and qualitative analysis, even in the questionnaires, is common to qualitative frameworks in which data from multiple sources, in diverse forms, are interwoven. In this study, the quantitative patterns that emerged from the questionnaires were examined as they were, but also were used to flag themes or questions that were further explored in the interviews. The reverse was also useful when the interview data were checked with numerical patterns for greater explanatory power.

TABLE 1. Characteristics of Questionnaire Respondents.

Variable	*N(%)*	
Age in years		
Under 25	9(7.1)	
25-34	49(38.6)	
35-44	38(29.9)	
45-54	24(18.9)	
55-64	7(5.5)	
Mean = 37.5 Range = 17-64		
Religion		
Protestant	64(57.1)	
Catholic	39(34.8)	
Jewish	9(8.0)	
Not listed	15 ——	
Educational level		
Less than high-school degree	4(3.1)	
High-school degree	41(32.3)	
Some college or training beyond high school	32(25.2)	
College degree	28(22.0)	
Some graduate training	4(3.1)	
Advanced degree	18(14.2)	
Marital status		
Married[1]	111(88.1)	
Divorced or separated	10(7.9)	
Widowed	3(2.4)	
Single (never married)	2(1.6)	
Not listed	1 ——	
Income		
Under $15,000	9(8.1)	
$15-25,000	39(35.1)	
$25,001-$35,000	26(23.4)	
$35,001-$45,000	18(16.2)	
$45,001-$55,000	13(11.7)	
Over $55,000	6(5.4)	
Not listed	16 ——	
Mean = $32,500$^+$ Range = $100,000$^+$		
Occupation[2]		
Homemaker only	57(46.0)	
Clerical/Sales	41(33.1)	*N* = 127
Professional	26(21.0)	

[1]It is the present marital status that is indicated and does not imply marriage to the same person as at the time of the child's death, or even the same marital status that existed at that time.

[2]Many of the women listed dual occupations of homemaker combined with an outside job. These were classified by occupation. Occupations requiring specialized training, such as R.N., were included in the Professional category.

TABLE 2. Characteristics of Interview Subjects.

Variable	*N(%)*
Age in years	
35-40	4(25.0)
41-45	4(25.0)
46-50	5(31.25)
51-55	1(6.25)
56-60	2(12.5)
N = 16 Mean = 45.6 Range = 36-57	
Religion	
Protestant	11(68.75)
Roman Catholic	4(25.0)
Jewish	1(6.25)
N = 16	
Educational level	
Less than high school degree	1(6.25)
High-school degree	2(12.5)
Some college or training beyond high school	5(31.25)
College degree	6(37.5)
Advanced degree	2(12.5)
N = 16	
Marital status	
Married[1]	16(100.0)
Income	
$15,000-$25,000	2(12.5)
$25,001-$35,000	3(18.8)
$35,001-$45,000	5(31.3)
$45,001-$55,000	3(18.8)
Over $55,000	2(12.5)
N = 16 Mean – $43,000+ Range = $20,000 - $10,000+	
Occupation[2]	
Homemaker only	4(25.0)
Clerical/Sales	8(50.0)
Professional	4(25.0)

[1]Two are second marriages, the separation occurring before the child's death.

[2]Three of those employed are working part time.

TABLE 3. Comparison of Questionnaire and Interview Respondents.

Variable	*Questionnaire Sample*	*Interview Subsample*
Mean age	37.5 years	45.6 years
Religion	57.1% Protestant	68.8% Protestant
Educational level	64.5% beyond high school	81.25% beyond high school
Marital status	88.1% married	100.0% married
Mean income	$32,500^{+}	$43,000^{+}
Occupation	54.1% employed	75% employed

As it turned out, of the 126 women who returned completed questionnaires, 54 were in the approximate age range designated for interviews. That number diminished because 12 filled out the questionnaire anonymously and an additional six said they would respond to further questionnaires but did not want to be interviewed. The two women who gave explanations cited poor health or "It's just too soon." In the latter case, the woman was contacted after a five-month interval but declined an interview. Five more women lived out of the state and were eliminated because of distance. Of the remaining 31 women who met the mothers' requirements, the cause of the child's death eliminated 13. Four of those deaths were suicides, two were infant mortalities, and seven deaths were as a result of congenital problems or long-term illness. Two more women were not contacted because the deaths were too far in the past for the purpose of this study; that left 16 women, 15 of whom were interviewed and one who said that she would call back after talking to her husband, but did not. This woman was the only one who expressed the need to discuss it before making an interview appointment and it may be partly explained by the fact that she had just remarried after being divorced for 13 years. The interview portion of the study, then, began with these 15 women, plus one who had been solicited from a different area.

TABLE 4. Time Elapsed Since Death of the Child.

Time Elapsed	*Frequency (%)*
0-1 year	28 (22.4)
1 year, 1 day-2 years	39 (31.2)
2 years, 1 day-3 years	24 (19.2)
3 years, 1 day-4 years	8 (6.4)
4 years, 1 day-5 years	7 (5.6)
Over 5 years	19 ——
Not listed	2 ——

Range = .17 years - 14.08 years Average = 2.5 years

TABLE 5. Women's Perceptions of Spouses' Importance Over Time.[1]

A. Before the death	$\bar{X}$ = 1.53; SD = 1.00;		*N* = 107
B. Year following the death	$\bar{X}$ = 1.71; SD = 1.28;		
	t = 1.82	r = .63	*N.S.*
B. Year following the death	$\bar{X}$ = 1.71; SD = 1.29;		*N* = 101
C. Now	X = 1.51; SD = 1.10;		
	t = 1.88	r = .62	*N.S.*
A. Before the death	$\bar{X}$ = 1.54; SD = 1.01;		N = 101
C. Now	$\bar{X}$ = 1.51; SD = 1.10;		
	t = .30	r = .57	*N.S.*

[1]In several of the tables, the *N*s differ because the scale was not completed. It was primarily because some women were still in the year following the death. Because of the different *N*s, the means are close but not identical.

TABLE 6. Women's Perceptions of Daughters' Importance Over Time.[1]

A. Before the death	$\bar{X}=1.27$; SD= .70;		*N*=55
B. Year following the death	$\bar{X}=1.09$; SD= .39;		
	t=1.80	r= .17	*N.S.*
B. Year following the death	$\bar{X}=1.09$; SD= .40;		*N*=52
C. Now	$\bar{X}=1.11$; SD= .42;		
	t= .29	r= .38	*N.S.*
A. Before the death	$\bar{X}=1.29$; SD= .71;		*N*=54
C. Now	$\bar{X}=1.11$; SD= .41;		
	t=2.46*	r= .64	

[1]See discussion of different *N*s and means in the footnote to Table 5.

**p* .05.

TABLE 7. Women's Perceptions of Sons' Importance Over Time.[1]

A. Before the death	$\bar{X}=1.44$; SD= .72;		*N*=58
B. Year following the death	$\bar{X}=1.17$; SD= .50;		
	t=2.34*	r= .02	
B. Year following the death	$\bar{X}=1.18$; SD= .51;		*N*=58
C. Now	$\bar{X}=1.20$; SD= .52;		
	t= .29	r= .63	*N.S.*
A. Before the death	$\bar{X}=1.44$; SD= .72;		*N*=58
C. Now	$\bar{X}=1.20$; SD= .52;		
	t=2.29*	r= .21	

[1]See discussion of different *N*s and means in the footnote to Table 5.

**p* .05.

TABLE 8. Women's Perceptions of Family's Importance Over Time[1] (Excludes Husband and Children).

A. Before the death	$\bar{X}=2.26$; SD = 1.17;			$N=253$
B. Year following the death	$\bar{X}=2.18$; SD = 1.37;			
		t = 1.05	r = .61	*N.S.*
B. Year following the death	$\bar{X}=2.29$; SD = 1.35;			$N=228$
C. Now	$\bar{X}=2.20$; SD = 1.28;			
		t = 1.29	r = .83	*N.S.*
A. Before the death	$\bar{X}=2.30$; SD = 1.17;			$N=228$
C. Now	$\bar{X}=2.21$; SD = 1.26;			
		t = 1.34	r = .64	*N.S.*

[1]See discussion of different *N*s and means in the footnote to Table 5.

TABLE 9. Women's Perceptions of Friends' Importance Over Time[1]

A. Before the death	$\bar{X}=2.80$; SD = 1.32			$N=330$
B. Year following the death	$\bar{X}=2.11$; SD = 1.21			
		t = 8.45*	r = .32	
B. Year following the death	$\bar{X}=2.08$; SD = 1.23			$N=310$
C. Now	$\bar{X}=2.43$; SD = 1.31			
		t = 6.21*	r = .69	
A. Before the death	$\bar{X}=2.58$; SD = 1.34			$N=212$
C. Now	$\bar{X}=2.51$; SD = 1.40			
		t = .57	r = .69	*N.S.*

[1]See discussion of different *N*s and means in the footnote to Table 5.

**p* .001

TABLE 10. Use of Professional Resources.[1]

N of Professionals Used	N of Women (%)	
0	27 (22.9)	
1	43 (36.4)	
2	33 (28.0)	
3	10 (8.5)	
4	4 (3.4)	
5	1 (.8)	*N*=118

[1]A total of 91 women (77.1 percent; *N*=118) reported using some form of professional help during this time, and 52.7 percent used more than one (Table 10). The most common combination was doctor and clergy, but 13 women used two doctors, four saw two clergy, and four noted two therapists.

TABLE 11. Women's Perceptions of Doctors' Importance Over Time.[1]

A. Before the death	$\bar{X}=2.76$; SD=1.33	*N*=51
B. Year following the death	$\bar{X}=2.70$; SD=1.47	
	t= .22 r= .09	*N.S.*
B. Year following the death	$\bar{X}=2.60$; SD=1.45	*N*=51
C. Now	$\bar{X}=3.03$; SD=1.53	
	t=3.06* r= .77	
A. Before the death	$\bar{X}=2.79$; SD=1.41	*N*=48
C. Now	$\bar{X}=3.08$; SD=1.55	*N.S.*
	t=1.17 r= .33	

[1]See discussion of different *N*s and means in the footnote to Table 5.

*p .001.

TABLE 12. Women's Perceptions of Clergy's Importance Over Time.[1]

A. Before the death	$\bar{X}=3.32$; SD = 1.50	$N=56$
B. Year following the death	$\bar{X}=2.42$; SD = 1.31	
	t = 4.25* r = .38	
B. Year following the death	$\bar{X}=2.44$; SD = 1.34	$N=52$
C. Now	$\bar{X}=3.03$; SD = 1.45	
	t = 3.94* r = .70	
A. Before the death	$\bar{X}=3.25$; SD = 1.53	$N=51$
C. Now	$\bar{X}=3.03$; SD = 1.46	
	t = .97 r = .44	*N.S.*

[1]See discussion of different *N*s and means in the footnote to Table 5.

*p .001.

TABLE 13. Women's Perceptions of Therapists' Importance Over Time.[1]

A. Before the death	$\bar{X}=3.81$; SD = 1.59	$N=22$
B. Year following the death	$\bar{X}=2.18$; SD = 1.36	
	t = 4.92* r = .45	
B. Year following the death	$\bar{X}=2.18$; SD = 1.36	$N=22$
C. Now	$\bar{X}=3.59$; SD = 1.59	
	t = 4.14* r = .42	
A. Before the death	$\bar{X}=3.85$; SD = 1.66	$N=22$
C. Now	$\bar{X}=3.75$; SD = 1.55	
	t = .28 r = .53	

[1]See discussion of different *N*s and means in the footnote to Table 5.

*p .001.

The increase in importance of therapeutic help was due to movement from low levels of importance to high levels, and the decrease was equally sharp.

TABLE 14. Attendance at Compassionate Friends Meetings.

Sample	Attendance at C.F.	N (%)	Total (%)
Self-help	Often	28 (22.0)	72 (56.7)
	Occasionally	44 (34.6)	
Nonmember	Once or twice	9 (7.1)	55 (43.3)
	Never	46 (36.2)	
		$N = 127$	

Questionnaire respondents were distinguished as group member or nonmember based on the self-reported criteria shown in Table 14, Attendance at Meetings of Compassionate Friends.

As seen in Table 14, those indicating Often or Occasionally constitute the Self-help portion of the sample, and those stating Once or Twice or Never are the Nonmembers. The distinction was not always clearcut. Six women who do not attend meetings reported elsewhere in the questionnaire that they have contact with that group through literature, individual Compassionate Friends' members, or that they attended another group of a similar nature. Eight more women who do not attend meetings singled out other bereaved mothers as special friends or supports. For purposes of this study, attendance at meetings will remain the distinguishing criterion, but the phenomenon of seeking out similar others as supports emerges here.

TABLE 15. Comparison of Self-help Group Members with Nonmembers.

Variable	*Self-help Group* *N*(%)		*Nonmember Group* *N*(%)	
Religion				
Protestant	36 (56.3)		27 (57.4)	
Roman Catholic	22 (34.4)		17 (36.2)	
Jewish	6 (9.4)		3 (6.4)	
Not listed	8 —		8 —	
		N=72		*N*=55
Number of children dead				
1	61 (84.7)		52 (94.5)	
2	8 (11.1)		3 (5.5)	
3	3 (4.2)		0 —	
		N=72		*N*=55
Gender of child				
Male	46 (63.4)		31 (59.6)	
Female	26 (36.6)		21 (40.4)	
Not listed	1 —		3 —	
		N=72		*N*=55
Occupation				
Homemaker only	29 (40.8)		28 (52.8)	
Clerical/sales	25 (35.2)		16 (30.2)	
Professional	17 (23.9)		9 (17.0)	
Not listed	1 —		2 —	
		N=72		*N*=55
Marital status				
Married	61 (85.9)		50 (90.0)	
Divorced/separated	8 (11.3)		2 (3.6)	
Widowed	2 (2.8)		1 (1.8)	
Single (never married)	0 —		2 (3.6)	
Not listed	1 —			
		N=72		*N*=55
Educational level				
Less than high-school degree	0 —		4 (7.3)	
High-school degree	25 (34.7)		16 (29.1)	
Some college or professional training	17 (23.6)		15 (27.3)	
College degree	14 (19.4)		14 (25.5)	
Some graduate training	3 (4.2)		1 (1.8)	
Advanced degree	13 (18.1)		5 (9.1)	
		N=72		*N*=55
Mean age in years	38.4	*N*=72	36.9	*N*=55
Mean income in thousands	30+		35+	
Mean time in years since death	2.8	*N*=69	2.08	*N*=54

Table 15 provides a comparison of group members and nonmembers along sociodemographic variables. More questions are raised from this comparison. The self-help group has higher percentages of women who have lost more than one child, are divorced or separated, and who work outside the home. Group members also have a higher mean age, income, and years elapsed since the death of the child. For this particular loss, it raises questions about whether younger women, because they can have more children (implying the future) are less likely to seek out a group for bereaved parents. Self-help groups are primarily used by younger populations, but loss of a child appears to encourage older mothers more than younger ones to seek this form of support.

TABLE 16. Cause of Death.

Group	*Accidents*[1]	*Early Death*[2]	*Cause Disease/ Illness*	*Homicide*	*Suicide*	
	N (%)	*N (%)*	*N (%)*	*N (%)*	*N (%)*	
Self-help	23 (31.9)	30 (41.7)	15 (20.8)	3 (4.2)	1 (1.4)	=72
Nongroup	21 (38.2)	24 (43.6)	5 (9.1)	0 —	5 (9.1)	=55
Total	44 (34.6)	54 (42.5)	20 (15.7)	3 (2.4)	6 (4.7)	127

[1]Accidents include plane crashes, car, truck, and motorcycle accidents, hanging, falling trees, asphyxiation, and drug overdose.

[2]Early deaths include miscarriage, stillborns, SIDS, birth complications if leading to early death, and congenital defects if leading to an early death.

The self-help group shows a higher proportion of mothers whose children died through disease and homicide, and a lower proportion of mothers whose children commited suicide. This study excluded interviews with mothers whose children had long illnesses, so data are not available to explain the difference.

Table 16 showed that mothers of children who committed suicide were underrepresented in the self-help group, but the numbers were very small. It was hypothesized at the outset of this study that suicides might engender more guilt than other deaths and were therefore eliminated from the interview sample. The trend toward nonparticipation in a group experience may have guilt as a factor; the mothers may not want to discuss and be reminded of the death.

The *interview* was the primary data-gathering strategy. It was a semistructured, open-ended, taped, 1½ to 2½ hour interview designed to elicit a description of the woman's *experience* of the mourning process and the events and feelings surrounding the death of her child. It was the subjective experience that this study aimed to capture and therefore the open-ended interview was the central tool.

The women were reminded at the outset that what they chose to share and to teach would be appreciated. This approach is in accord with Benny and Hughes' philosophy of the interview as an interaction that encourages equality of the two participants by the interviewer's willingness to accept the affect and information that the respondent has to offer, minimizing interviewer differences and preconceived notions.[1]

The interviews began with questions about the child and the circumstances of the death. There was a clear alignment with respondents in identifying their experience as a major loss. As the interview progressed, there were opportunities to probe for ambivalent feelings about the child and to explore the coping and recovery portion of the process as well as the loss. Statements expressing ambivalence were accepted with the underlying belief that there were a range of emotions involved in the process. The general position of the interviewer was one of alliance with the respondent, not opposition. Challenges to statements offered were in the form of "I wonder if . . ." and rephrasing questions to approach other facets of the topics discussed.

Benny and Hughes also state that "information is the more valued the more freely given," encouraging a contract based on a flowing conversation rather than an approach bordering on cross-examination.[2] In this study, there were certainly questions that were asked and issues to be covered, but they were done in different sequence and with different emphasis, depending on the interviewee, what was volunteered, and with a sensitivity to the access each individual respondent had to her own emotional life.

Analysis of Interview Data

The information derived from the interview was analyzed based on the principles of Grounded Theory by Glaser and Strauss.[3] This is the process by which theory can be systematically obtained and analyzed through joint collection and coding procedures.

Theory in this sense refers to a way of handling data, providing modes of conceptualization for describing and explaining findings clearly enough to be verified in present and future research.

Glaser and Strauss describe whereby evidence, or facts, emerge first from the data as interviews and related observations.[4] These facts lead, secondly, to conceptual categories or their properties, which are theoretical abstractions that can be made based on the facts. The conceptual categories are the structures that support the data. The properties that conceptual categories must include are:

1. They must be central in relating facts and be able to include variations that appear in data;
2. They are illustrative through examples occurring regularly in the data;
3. They allow both experience and events to be interwoven;
4. They provide a great deal of explanatory power.

The process, then, proceeds from evidence to conceptual categories and, thirdly, to relationships among conceptual categories that allow the generation of theory.

Generating theory not only implies that many hypotheses and concepts come from the data, but also that they are worked out in relation to the data during the process of research. The "constant comparative method" of quantitative analysis means that

> . . . joint collection, coding and analysis of the data is the underlying operation. The generation of theory coupled with the notion of theory as process requires that all operations be done together as much as possible. They should blur and intertwine continually from beginning to end.[5]

Continuous analysis implies that indigenous themes can be tested on other subjects to see if there is a regularity of ideas and consistency that allows classification of people, events, and stages. In this study, for example, facts collected from interviews and questionnaires were checked out during subsequent interviews, and fleeting or incomplete ideas were further inquired about at that time or later. This is also true of facts that come from readings, additional fieldwork, other sources, and personal wonderings. All are subject to additional exploration before accepting or discarding them as conceptual properties. Theoretical sampling, the notion that emerging theory *controls* the lines of data collection, insists on procedures whereby comparative data, emerging from progressions of interviews and complementary practices, is continually checked and modified until saturated. The product is a tapestry woven together to form the final fabric.

As we previously implied, the analysis of quantitative data is not through use of magical insight, but a systematic discovery of significant classes of things, persons, and events and the properties which characterize and link them.

The interviews focused on a schedule of topics, but questions were not always asked the same way or in the same order. The dialogue was based on the process of theoretical sampling in which lines of thought were pursued as they emerged in one or a series of interviews. Theoretical sampling encourages the decision of where to go next as being based on emerging data and stopping when lines of thought have been saturated by a series of interviews.[6]

Specific comparisons were made to search out similarities and differences. The data were primarily compared along sociodemographic dimensions of the questionnaire and use of support systems. Other specific comparisons were made within the interview sample between the subjects who used self-help groups and those who did not. The self-help group versus the non self-help group was the only forced group delineation. Other patterns emerged, aiding the understanding of inconsistencies as well as areas of generalization.

NOTES

1. Mark Benny and Everett Hughes, "Of Sociology and the Interview," *American Journal of Sociology, 62* (1956): 137-142.

2. Ibid., p. 139.

3. Barney Glaser and Anselm Strauss, *The Discovery of Grounded Theory: Strategies for Qualitative Research* (New York: Aldine, 1967).

4. Ibid.

5. Ibid., p. 43.

6. Ibid.

Bibliography

Abraham, K. Object-loss and introjection in normal mourning and in abnormal states of mind. In *Selected papers of Karl Abraham,* New York: Basic Books, 1927, 433-443. (Originally published, 1924)

Ackerman, N. Disturbances of mothering and criteria for treatment. *American Journal of Orthopsychiatry,* 1956, *26* (2), 252-263.

Alexy, W. Dimensions of psychological counseling that facilitate the grieving process of bereaved parents, *Journal of Counseling Psychology, 29,* no.5 (1982): 498-507.

Anderson, C. Aspects of pathological grief and mourning. *International Journal of Psychoanalysis,* 1949, *30,* 48-55.

Antonucci, T., and Depner, C. Conceptual and methodological issues. In L. Troll (Chair), *Social support through the life course.* Symposium presented at the 88th annual meeting of the American Psychological Association, Montreal, September 1980.

Balint, A. Love for the mother and mother-love. In M. Balint (ed.), *Primary love and psychoanalytic technique.* London: Hogarth Press, 1952, 109-127. (Originally published, 1939).

Bart, P. Depression in middle-age women. In V. Gornick (ed.), *Women in sexist society.* New York: Basic Books, 1971, 99-117.

Becker, E. *The denial of death.* New York: The Free Press, 1973.

Benedek, T. Psychobiological aspects of mothering. *American Journal of Orthopsychiatry,* 1956, *26* (2), 272-278.

Benedek, T. Parenthood as a developmental phase. *Journal of the American Psychological Association,* 1959, *7* (3), 389-417.

Benny, M., and Hughes, E. Of sociology and the interview: Editorial preface. *American Journal of Sociology,* 1956, *(62),* 137-142.

Bibring, E. The mechanisms of depression. In P. Greenacre (ed.), *Affective disorders.* New York: International Universities Press, 1953.

Binswanger, L. *Sigmund Freud: Reminiscences of a friendship.* New York: Grune and Stratton, 1957.

Blum, H. The maternal ego ideal and the regulation of maternal qualities. In S. Greenspan and G. Pollock (eds.), *The course of life: psychoanalytic contributions toward understanding personality development* (Vol. 3). (U.S. Department of Health and Human Services). Washington, D.C.: U.S. Government Printing Office, 1981, 91-114.

Blumer, H. Methodological principles of empirical science. In N. Denzin (ed.), *Sociological methods: a sourcebook.* Chicago: Aldine, 1970, 20-39.

Borman, L. Characteristics of development and growth. In M. Lieberman, L. Borman, and Associates, *Self-help groups for coping with crisis.* San Francisco: Jossey-Bass, 1979, 13-42.

Bowlby, J. Grief and mourning in infancy and early childhood. *The Psychoanalytic Study of the Child,* 1960, *15,* 9-52.

Bowlby, J. Process of mourning. *International Journal of Psychoanalysis,* 1961, *42,* 317-340.

Brown, B. Social and psychological correlates of help-seeking behavior among urban adults. *American Journal of Community Psychology,* 1978, *6* (5), 425-439.

Cain, A., and Cain, B. On replacing a child. *Journal of the American Academy of Child Psychiatrists,* 1964, *3,* 443-456.

Carr, A. Bereavement as a relative experience. In B. Schoenberg, (ed.), *Bereavement: its psychosocial aspects.* New York: Columbia University Press, 1975, 3-8.

Chodoff, P., Friedman, S., Hamburg, D. Stress, defenses and coping behavior: observations in parents of children with malignant disease. *American Journal of Psychiatry,* 1964, *120,* 743-749.

Chodorow, N. *The reproduction of mothering: psychoanalysis and the sociology of gender.* Berkeley: University of California Press, 1978.

Clayton, P., Desmarais, L., and Winoker, G. A study of normal bereavement. *American Journal of Psychiatry,* 1968, *125,* 168-178.

Clayton, P. The sequelae and nonsequelae of conjugal bereavement. *American Journal of Psychiatry,* 1979, *136,* 1530-1534.

Cobb, S. A model for life events and their consequences. In B.S. Dohrenwend and B.P. Dohrenwend (eds.), *Stressful life events: Their nature and effects.* New York: John Wiley & Sons, 1974, 151-156.

Cobb, S. Social support as a moderator of life stress. *Psychosomatic Medicine,* 1976, *38* (5), 300-313.

Davidson, G. *Understanding: Death of the wished-for child.* OGR Service Corporation, Springfield, IL, 1979.

Degner, L. Death in disaster: Implications for bereavement. *Essence,* 1976, *1,* 69-77.

Deutsch, H. Absence of grief. *Psychoanalytic Quarterly,* 1937, *6,* 12-22.

Dexter, L. Role relationships and conceptions of neutrality in interviewing. *American Journal of Sociology,* 1956, *62,* 153-164.

Engel, G. Is grief a disease? *Psychosomatic Medicine,* 1961, *23* (1), 18-22.

Engel, G. *Psychological development in health and disease.* Philadelphia: W.B. Saunders, 1962.

Engel, G. A life setting conducive to illness. *Bulletin of the Menninger,* 1968, *32,* 335-365.

Engel, G., and Schmale, A. Psychoanalytic theory of somatic disorder. *Journal of the American Psychoanalytic Association,* 1967, *15,* 344-363.

Erikson, E. *Childhood and society* (2nd ed.). New York: Norton, 1963.

Erikson, E. *Identity: Youth and crisis.* New York: Norton, 1968.

Erikson, K. *Everything in its path.* New York: Simon and Schuster, 1976.

Feifel, H. *New meanings of death.* New York: McGraw Hill, 1977.

Festinger, L., and Katz, D. *Research methods in the behavioral sciences.* New York: Dryden Press, 1953.

Freud, A. Adolescence. *Psycho-analytic Study of the Child,* 1958, *13,* 255-278.

Freud, S. New introductory lectures on psychoanalysis (1932). New York: Norton, 1933.

Freud, S. On narcissism. *Standard Edition.* London: Hogarth Press, 1957, *14,* 67-104 (Originally published, 1914).

Freud, S. On transience. *Standard Edition.* London: Hogarth Press, 1957, *14,* 303-307. (Originally published, 1916).

Freud, S. Mourning and melancholia. In E. Jones (ed.), *Sigmund Freud: collected papers.*New York: Basic Books, 1959. (Originally published, 1917).

Freud, S. The ego and the id. *Standard Edition.* London: Hogarth Press, 1961, *19,* 3-68. (Originally published, 1923).

Frieberg, P., and Bridwell, M. An intervention model for rape and unwanted pregnancy. *Counseling Psychologist,* 1976, *6,* 50-53.

Fried, M. Grieving for a lost home. In Duhl (ed.), *The environment of the metropolis.* New York: Basic Books, 1962.

Glaser, B., and Strauss, A. *The discovery of grounded theory: Strategies for qualitative research.* Chicago: Aldine Press, 1967.

Glick, I., Weiss, R., and Parkes, C. *The first year of bereavement.* New York: John Wiley and Sons, 1974.

Goin, M., Burgoyne, R.W., and Goin, J. Timeless attachment to a dead relative. *American Journal of Psychiatry,* 1979, *136* (7), 988-989.

Gorer, G. *Death, grief and mourning.* London: Cresset Press, 1965.

Gould, R. *Transformations.* New York: Simon and Schuster, 1978.

Gourash, N. Help-Seeking: A review of the literature. *American Journal of Psychology,* 1978, *6* (5), 413-423.

Grand, H. Fear of becoming insane. *American Journal of Psychotherapy,* 1959, *13* (1), 51-54.

Greene, W. Role of a vicarious object in adaptation to object loss. *Psychosomatic Medicine,* 1958, *20* (5), 344-350.

Gurin, G., Veroff, J., and Feld, S. *Americans view their mental health: A nationwide survey.* New York: Basic Books, 1960.

Gut, E. Some aspects of adult mourning. *Omega,* 1974, *5* (4), 323-340.

Hamburg, D., Coelho, G., and Adams, J. *Coping and adaptation.* New York: Basic Books, 1974.

Hodgkinson, P. Abnormal grief—the problem of therapy. *British Journal of Medical Psychology,* 1982, 55, 29-34.

Horowitz, M., Wilner, N., Marmar, C., and Krupnick, J. Pathological grief and the activation of latent self-images. *American Journal of Psychiatry,* 1980, *137* (10), 1152-1162.

Janis, I. *Psychological Stress.* New York: John Wiley and Sons, 1958.

Janis, I. Psychological effects of warnings. In Baker (ed.), *Man and society in disaster.* New York: Basic Books, 1962.

Jaques, E. Death and the mid-life crisis. *International Journal of Psychoanalysis,* 1965, *46,* 502-514.

Kardiner, A. Traumatic neuroses of war. *American Handbook of Psychiatry,* 1959, *1,* 246-257.

Kennell, J., Slyter, H., and Klaus, M. The mourning response of parents to the death of a newborn infant. *New England Journal of Medicine,* 1970, *283* (7), 344-349.

Kernberg, O. *Internal world and external reality.* New York: Jason Aronson, 1980.

Krupp, G. The bereavement reaction. *Psychoanalytic Study of Society* (Vol.2). New York: International Universities Press, 1962, 42-74.

Lampl-de Groot, J. On adolescence. *Psycho-analytic study of the child,* 1960, *13,* 95-103.

Lieberman, M. The effects of social supports on responses to stress. In L. Goldberger and S. Breznitz (eds.), *Handbook of stress.* New York: Free Press, 1981.

Lieberman, M., Borman, L., and Associates. *Self-help groups for coping with crisis.* San Francisco: Jossey-Bass, 1979.

Lieberman, S. Nineteen cases of morbid grief. *British Journal of Psychiatry,* 1978, *132,* 159-163.

Liefer, M. *Psychological effects of motherhood: A study of first pregnancy.* New York: Praeger, 1980.

Lifton, R. *The broken connection: On death and the continuity of life.* New York: Simon and Schuster, 1979.

Lindemann, E. Symptomatology and management of acute grief. *American Journal of Psychiatry,* 1944, *101,* 141-148.

Loewald, H. Internalization, separation, mourning and the superego. *Psychoanalytic Quarterly,* 1962, *31,* 483-504.

Lowenthal, M., and Haven, C. Interaction and adaptation: Intimacy, a critical variable. *American Sociological Review,* 1968, *33,* Part 1, 20-30.

Maddison, D., and Viola, A. The health of widows in the year following bereavement. *Journal of Psychosomatic Research,* 1968, *12,* 297-306.

Marris, P. *Loss and change.* London: Routledge and Kegan Paul, 1975.

McGough, J. Hormonal influences on memory storage. *American Psychologist,* 1983, *38* (2), 161-173.

Myers, J., Lindenthal, J., and Pepper, M. Life events, social integration and psychiatric symptomatology. *Journal of Health and Social Behavior,* 1975, *16,* 421-431.

Neugarten, B., and Datan, N. The midlife years. In S. Arieti (ed.), *American handbook of psychiatry*(Vol. 1, 2nd ed.). New York: Basic Books, 1974, 592-608.

Niederland, W. The survivor syndrome: further observations and dimensions. *Journal of the American Psychoanalytic Association,* 1981, *29* (2), 413-426.

Nuckolls, K., Cassel, J., and Kaplan, B. Psychosocial assets, life crises, and the prognosis of pregnancy. *American Journal of Epidemiology,* 1972, *95,* 431-441.

Orbach, C. The multiple meanings of the loss of a child. *American Journal of Psychotherapy,* 1959, *13* (4), 906-915.

Parkes, C.M. The first year of bereavement: A longitudinal study of the reactions of London widows to the death of their husbands. *Psychiatry,* 1970, *33,* 444-467.

Parkes, C.M. *Bereavement: Studies of grief in adult life.* New York: International Universities Press, 1972.

Parkes, C.M. Unexpected and untimely bereavement: A statistical study of young Boston widows and widowers. In B. Schoenberg, I. Gerber, A. Weiner, A. Kutscher, D. Peretz, and A. Carr (eds.), *Bereavement: Its psychosocial aspects.* New York: Columbia University Press, 1975, 119-138.

Parkes, C.M. Bereavement counseling: Does it work? *British Medical Journal,* July 1980, 3-6.

Parkes, C.M., and Brown, R. Health after bereavement: A controlled study of young Boston widows and widowers. *Psychosomatic Medicine,* 1972, *34,* 449-460.

Peretz, D. Development, object relationships and loss. In B. Schoenberg, A. Carr, D. Peretz, and A. Kutscher (eds.), *Loss and grief: Psychological management in medical practice.* New York: Columbia University Press, 1970, 3-19.

Peretz, D. Reaction to loss. In B. Schoenberg, A. Carr, D. Peretz, and A. Kutscher (eds.), *Loss and Grief: psychological management in medical practice.* New York: Columbia University Press, 1970, 20-35.

Pollock, G. Mourning and adaptation. *International Journal of Psychoanalysis, 1961, 42,* 341-361.

Pollock, G. On symbiosis and symbiotic neurosis. *International Journal of Psychoanalysis,* 1964, *45,* 1-30.

Pollock, G. Temporal anniversary manifestations: hour, day, holiday. *Psychoanalytic Quarterly, 40,* no.1 (1971): 123-131.

Pollock, G. On mourning and anniversaries: The relationship of culturally constituted defensive systems to intropsychic adaptive processes. *Israel Annals of Psychiatry,* 1972, *10* (1), 9-40.

Pollock, G. On mourning, immortality, and utopia. *Journal of the American Psychoanalytic Association,* 1975, *23* (2), 334-362.

Pollock, G. Manifestations of abnormal mourning: homicide and suicide following the death of another. *The Annual of Psychoanalysis,* 1976, *4,* 225-249.

Pollock, G. Process and affect: mourning and grief. *International Journal of Psychoanalysis,* 1978, *59,* 255-276.

Ramsay, R., and Happee, J. The stress of bereavement: components and treatment. In I. Sarason (ed.), *Stress and Anxiety* (Vol.4), London: John Wiley and Sons, 1977.

Raphael, B. Preventive intervention with the recently bereaved. *Archives of General Psychiatry,* 1977, *34,* 1450-1454.

Romm, M. Loss of sexual function in the female.In B. Schoenberg, A. Carr, D. Peretz, and A. Kutscher (eds.), *Loss and grief: Psychological management in medical practice.* New York: Columbia University Press, 1970, 178-188.

Rubin, L. *Women of a certain age.* New York: Harper & Row, 1979.

Sanders, C. A comparison of adult bereavement in the death of a spouse, child and parent. *Omega,* 1979-1980, *10* (4), 303-321.

Schacter, S. *The psychology of affiliation.* Stanford, California: Stanford University Press, 1959.

Schafer, R. *Aspects of internalization.* New York: International Universities Press, 1968.

Schmale, A. Giving up as a final common pathway to changes in health. *Advances in Psychosomatic Medicine,* 1972, *8,* 20-40.

Schmale, A., and Engel, G. The giving up-given up complex. *Archives of General Psychiatry,* 1967, *17,* 135-145.

Schoenberg, B., Gerber, I., Wiener, A., Kutscher, A., Peretz, D., and Carr, A. (eds.). *Bereavement: Its psychosocial aspects.* New York: Columbia University Press, 1975.

Sherman, B. Emergence of ideology in a bereaved parents group. In M. Lieberman, L. Borman, and Associates, *Self-help groups for coping with crisis.* San Francisco: Jossey-Bass, 1979, 305-322.

Singh, B. and Raphael, B. Postdisaster morbidity of the bereaved: A possible role for preventive psychiatry? *Journal of Nervous and Mental Disease,* 1981, *169* (4), 203-212.

Smith, J. Identificatory styles in depression and grief. *International Journal of Psychoanalysis,* 1971, *52,* 259-266.

Stern, K., Williams, G., and Prados, M. Grief reactions in later life. *American Journal of Psychiatry,* 1951, *108,* 289-294.

Volkan, V., Ciluffo, A.F., and Sarvay, T.L. Re-grief therapy and the function of the linking object as a key to stimulate emotionality. In *Emotional Flooding.* P. Olsen (ed.). New York: Human Sciences Press, 1976.

Warheit, G. Life events, coping, stress and depressive symptomatology. *American Journal of Psychiatry,* 1979, *136,* 413-507.

White, R. Strategies of adaptation: an attempt at systematic description. In R. Moos (ed.), *Human Adaptation: Coping with Life Crises.* Lexington, MA: Heath, 1976.

Wittkower, E. Rehabilitation of the limbless: Joint surgical and psychological study. *Occupational Medicine,* 1947, *3,* 20-34.

Wolfenstein, M. *Disaster: A psychological essay.* Glencoe, IL: Free Press, 1957.

Wolfenstein, M. How is mourning possible? *Psychoanalytic Study of the Child,* 1966, *21,* 93-123.

Worden, J.W. *Grief counseling and grief therapy.* New York: Springer, 1982.

Index

—•—

About the Author

Linda Edelstein received her Ph.D. from Northwestern University, and has a private practice in Evanston, Illinois.